Lancaster

Written by Ron Mackay

Walk Around

Squadron/Signal Publications

Cover Art by Don Greer
Profile Art by Tom Tullis
Line Illustrations by Melinda Turnage

(Front Cover) The Avro Lancaster was first unveiled to the British public on 28 August 1942. The chosen aircraft was VN: N / R5689 from No. 50 Sqdn., operating within No. 5 Group, RAF Bomber Command. Less than a month later, on 19 September, the aircraft was "written off," following a crash-landing after a "gardening" (mine-laying) operation.

(Back Cover) A Lancaster Mk. I (Special) with No. 617 "Dambusters" Sqdn. carries a 22,000-lb. "Grand Slam" aerodynamic bomb. The massive girth of the bomb required the removal of the bomb bay doors from all aircraft assigned to this specific duty. PD119 / YZ: J wears the "day" camouflage pattern applied to these particular squadron aircraft.

About the Walk Around®/On Deck Series®

The Walk Around®/On Deck® series is about the details of specific military equipment using color and black-and-white archival photographs and photographs of in-service, preserved, and restored equipment. *Walk Around®* titles are devoted to aircraft and military vehicles, while *On Deck®* titles are devoted to warships. They are picture books of 80 pages, focusing on operational equipment, not one-off or experimental subjects.

Copyright 2010 Squadron/Signal Publications
1115 Crowley Drive, Carrollton, TX 75006-1312 U.S.A.
Printed in the U.S.A.

All rights reserved. No part of this publication may be reproduced, stored in a retrieval system, or transmitted in any form by means electrical, mechanical, or otherwise, without written permission of the publisher.

ISBN 978-0-89747-616-4

Military/Combat Photographs and Snapshots

If you have any photos of aircraft, armor, soldiers, or ships of any nation, particularly wartime snapshots, please share them with us and help make Squadron/Signal's books all the more interesting and complete in the future. Any photograph sent to us will be copied and returned. Electronic images are preferred. The donor will be fully credited for any photos used. Please send them to:

Squadron/Signal Publications
1115 Crowley Drive
Carrollton, TX 75006-1312 U.S.A.
www.SquadronSignalPublications.com

(Title Page) A CWH Lancaster banks for the crowd at the annual "Thunder over Michigan" event at Willow Run Airport in Belleville on 18 July 2009. (Rich Kolasa)

Acknowledgments

This book would not have been possible without the generous help of Martin Bowman, Norman Didwell, Harry Holmes, Ron Liversage, John D. R. Rawlings, Bruce Robertson, and Jerry Scutts.

The author extends his particular thanks to the Panton brothers, proud owners of the NX611, which they maintain as a practical memorial to their elder brother Chris who was killed in action with Bomber Command during the disastrous Nuremberg raid of 30/31 March 1944. Grateful thanks are further extended to S/Ldr. Paul Day (in charge of the B of B Memorial Flight) for a fine guided tour of PA474. Finally, Linda Mason of the IWM staff, Duxford, is to be thanked for granting regular access to KB889.

Introduction

The Avro Lancaster was unquestionably the finest all-round performer during the bombing campaign waged by the British Royal Air Force (RAF) Bomber Command and targeted on the Nazi empire between 1942 and 1945. No fewer than 156,000 individual sorties were flown and over 600,000 tons of explosives and incendiaries deposited upon the enemy's industrial and military base.

Whatever the merits and demerits of nocturnal bombing raids, there is little doubt that the Lancaster played a leading role in hammering home the lesson to the Nazi hierarchy that its efforts to dominate Europe were doomed to ultimate failure, as the Allied strategic bombers applied their inexorable pressure "round the clock." (The fact that the author's uncle survived 36 "ops" [missions] as a bomb aimer with No. 49 Squadron should not be regarded as showing too much bias in favor of Avro's mighty machine!)

The contemporary photographs included in this volume feature three Lancasters, one of which shares with a Canadian-based "cousin" the honor of being the only examples of Roy Chadwick's splendid design that still take to the air. The main aircraft featured is also a Canadian-constructed airframe – KB889, a Mk. X that saw active service during World War II (WWII), but which resides in static honor at the Imperial War Museum in Duxford. The second aircraft is NX611, a Mk. VII that appeared too late to go on operations, but is maintained in ground running order at East Kirkby, where Lancasters of Nos. 57 and 630 Squadrons once launched their nightly raids on Germany.

PA474 was also too late to participate actively in WWII, but today, she forms the kernel of the RAF's Battle of Britain Memorial Flight (BBMF), appearing in the skies along with the Flight's fine collection of Hurricanes and Spitfires at various venues every summer. The deep resonance of her four Merlin engines as her distinctive aerodynamic shape thunders overhead serves as a fine and poignant reminder of the multitude of RAF and Commonwealth airmen (among whose ranks were many Americans) who rode the night skies over Germany and paved the way for final Victory, albeit at the cost of fully 55,000 from among their ranks.

The Lancaster remained in front-line service with Bomber Command until 1950 and Coastal Command until 1956. In addition, numerous individual airframes served as engine test-beds. Finally, a transport version utilizing the Lancaster's wing and tail structure – the Avro York – was introduced during WWII. Ironically its finest hour occurred during the Soviet land blockade of West Berlin in 1948/49, when the RAF and USAF successfully supplied the citizens of that city with all essential food and materials.

Dedication

This book is dedicated to the 55,000 RAF, Commonwealth, and other nations' personnel (including many from the USA) of Bomber Command, who rode the deadly night skies over Europe and never lived to savor the precious gift of freedom. They faced-up to and helped to put down the evils of autocracy, surrendering their lives in the process. Never forget what they achieved for their own as well as future generations.

Rear fuselage sections await the next step of the production process in the Lancaster production line. Rectangular gaps close to the rear turrets are the stabilizer slots. Sliding panels in the upper-central turret Plexiglas provide the gunners with enhanced visibility. "Arrow-head" shapes are the "Monica" aerials for detecting approaching aircraft.

PA474 passes low over the ground with the main undercarriage in the fully extended position The squadron code letters PM denote a bomber serving with No.103 Sqdn. and stand out clearly against the gloss black fuselage surface.

This view of PA474 on the ground displays the solid and purposeful outline of the Lancaster as well as the great length of the bomb-bay doors that are shown in the open position. Aircraft camouflage scheme is the standard one generally applied to the Avro four-engine bomber – dark green and dark earth on the upper wing and stabilizer/elevator surfaces and top edges of the fuselage and black on the remainder of the aircraft surfaces.

PA474 has been re-painted with the markings of several squadrons during its service with the BBMF. This fine example relates to an aircraft that flew with No. 9 Squadron (WS: J) and carries the slogan and artwork for a famous brand of Scotch whiskey. The bomb-aimer's Plexiglas blister is now the later pattern, with a deeper overall shape and the optical flat at a shallower angle.

The white color on the vertical fin on PA474 is believed to have been applied in mid-1944 on No. 9 Squadron bombers equipped with the "G-H" radio navigation system.

"H" pattern aerials on PA474 are mounted on both sides of the nose and are part of the aircraft's blind-landing equipment code-named *Rebecca*. The bomb-aimer's Plexiglas blister is the original shallow shape fitted on early-production Lancasters. The circular optical flat is raised at a sharper angle compared to that on the blister design introduced later in WWII.

The WS: J artwork is seen in closer detail. The impressive operations "tally" of symbols is applied in yellow for night sorties and white for day. The left hand column includes medal awards to the crew. The yellow swastika in the middle denotes a night fighter "kill."

PA474's current markings relate to a No. 61 Squadron Lancaster QR: M named *Minnie the Moocher*. Yellow edges on code letters and repetition of aircraft letter on the vertical fin were features on bombers serving in No. 5 Group from mid-1944 onwards.

NX611 is a late-production Lancaster Mk. VII that saw no active service. It is capable of operating under its own power but only for taxiing purposes. The artwork depicts *Just Jane,* a popular cartoon character in a wartime British newspaper. The family that owns the aircraft also farms part of the former airfield at East Kirkby, Lincolnshire, from where Lancasters of Nos. 57 and 630 Sqdn. operated during WWII.

Close view of the forward cockpit frame on PA474 picks out the curved horizontal frame on the side windshield panel. The small Plexiglas section above the curved frame opens to provide a "clear vision" facility.

The Lancaster's forward cockpit canopy consists of welded steel tubular frames bolted onto the die-cast windscreen. The rear section of the canopy tapers inwards and is formed from spruce. The canopy frames were all sprayed in dark-earth color prior to the fitting of the complete canopy, as can be clearly seen in this picture of NX611.

KB889 is a Canadian-built Mk. X Lancaster. This aircraft, unlike PA474 and NX611, did see action during WWII with No. 428 "Ghost" Sqdn. in No. 6 (Canadian) Group, and wears the code letters used at that time. She now resides as a prize possession of the Imperial War Museum (IWM) at Duxford, Cambridgeshire.

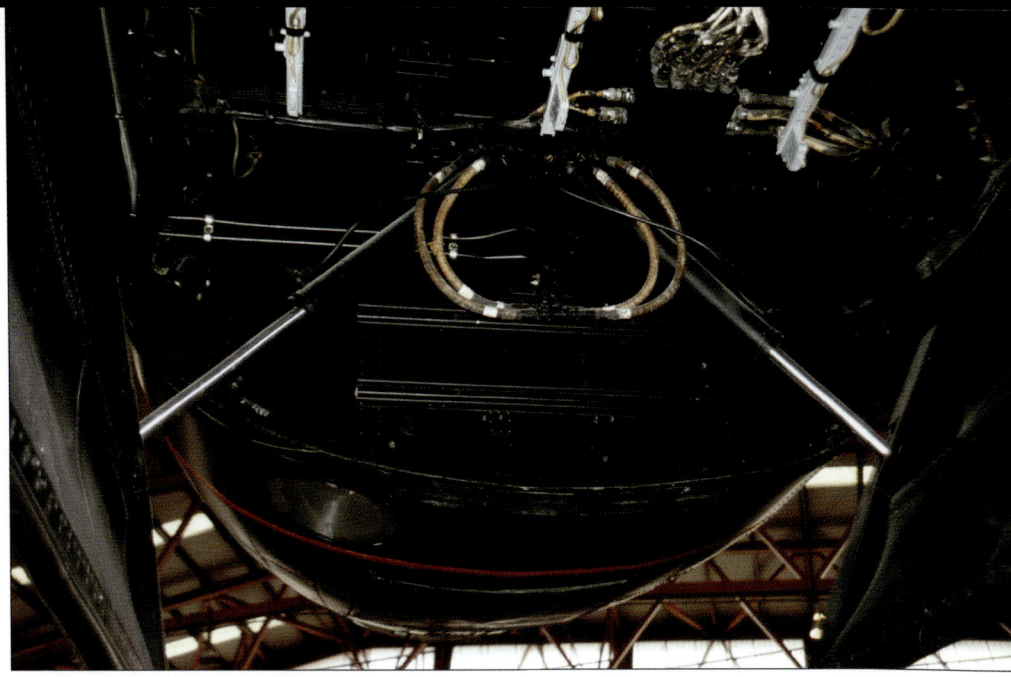

The bomb bay doors are operated with pairs of retractable support rods. The rods are natural metal and slide into and out of the black tubes attached to the bomb bay roof. This picture of the forward bulkhead also reveals the double curved interior surfaces of the bomb bay doors. The entire bomb bay area was sprayed black.

Adjacent to the rear bomb bay bulkhead is the rear pair of the bomb door retraction rods. Circular windows at the top of bulkhead allow the bomb aimer to confirm whether or not all bombs have been properly released.

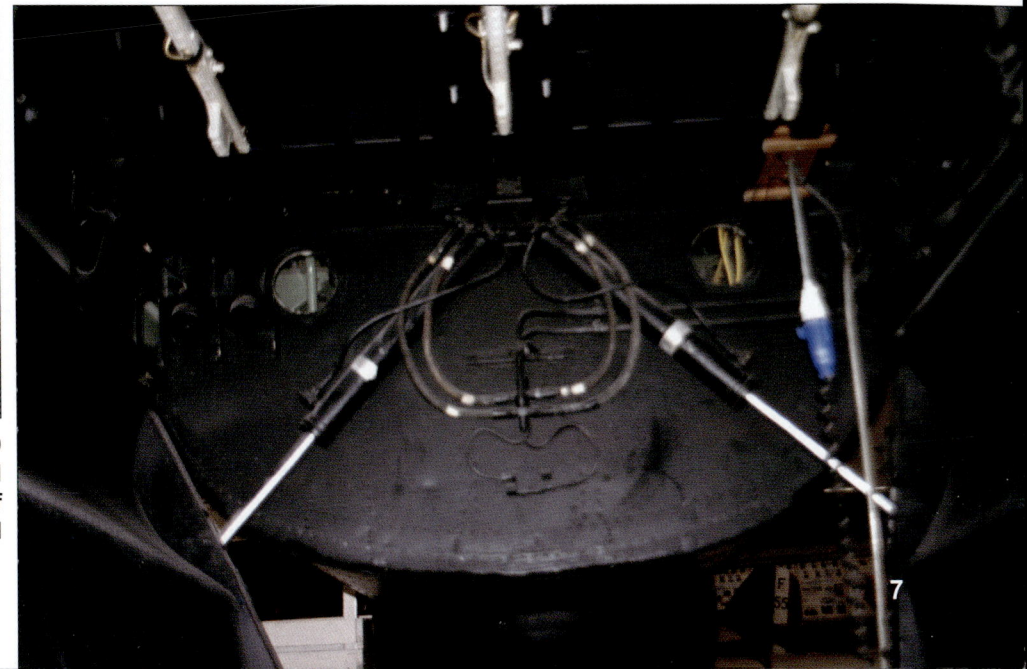

The Lancaster's massive bomb bay is 33 feet long – nearly half the fuselage length of 69 ft. 6 in. – and consists of a single open area. The standard bomb load usually consisted of a single 4,000-lb. high-explosive bomb known as a "cookie" along with a mixture of 1,000-lb. and 500-lb. bombs as well as incendiary containers. The maximum bomb load was 18,000 lbs.

The fixed bomb "crutches" positioned in the center of the Lancaster's bomb bay were used for the larger-sized bombs. The most commonly used was the 4,000-lb. blast bomb known as a "cookie." The largest bomb carried internally by the Lancaster was the 12,000-lb. aerodynamic weapon known as "Tallboy," which was used to sink the German battleship *Tirpitz* in November 1944. The "crutches" are colored red.

A large Plexiglas cover facilitated the bomb aimer's task. The optically flat circle in the center is used for focusing the bombsight. The rectangular Plexiglas panel directly under the bomber's nose provides additional visual reference for the bomb aimer.

Inside KB889's bomb bay are flexible bomb-support frames, two of which are seen here. The support frames were lowered on cables, attached to a bomb and then winched back up into the bomb bay.

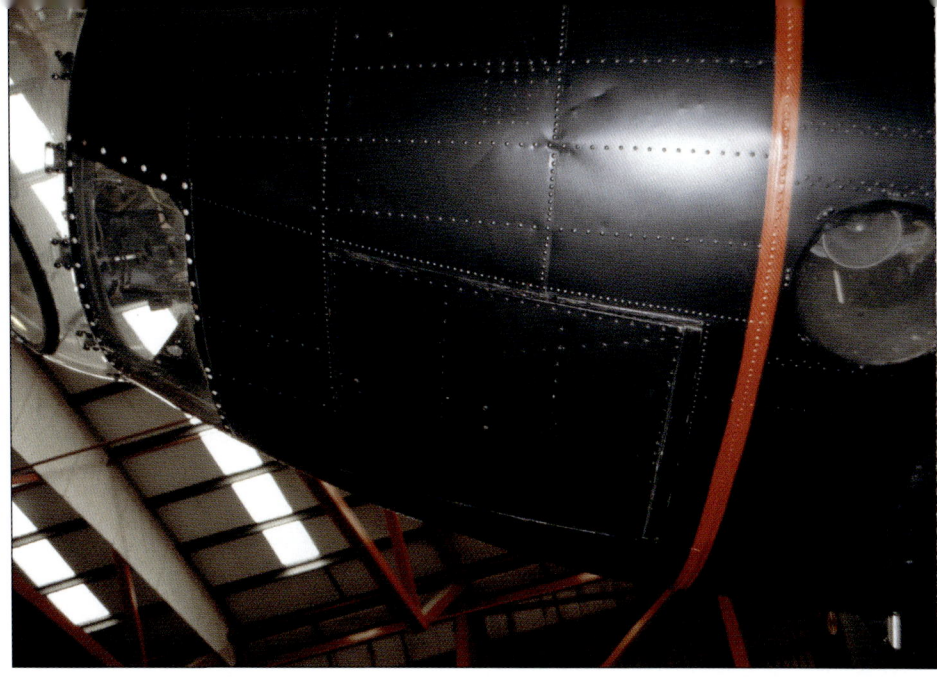

An external view of the nose underside shows the rectangular outline of the main escape hatch in the bomb aimer's compartment. The red line marks the location for the forward trestle-support when raising the Lancaster off its landing gear.

Bomb Aimer's Bubble

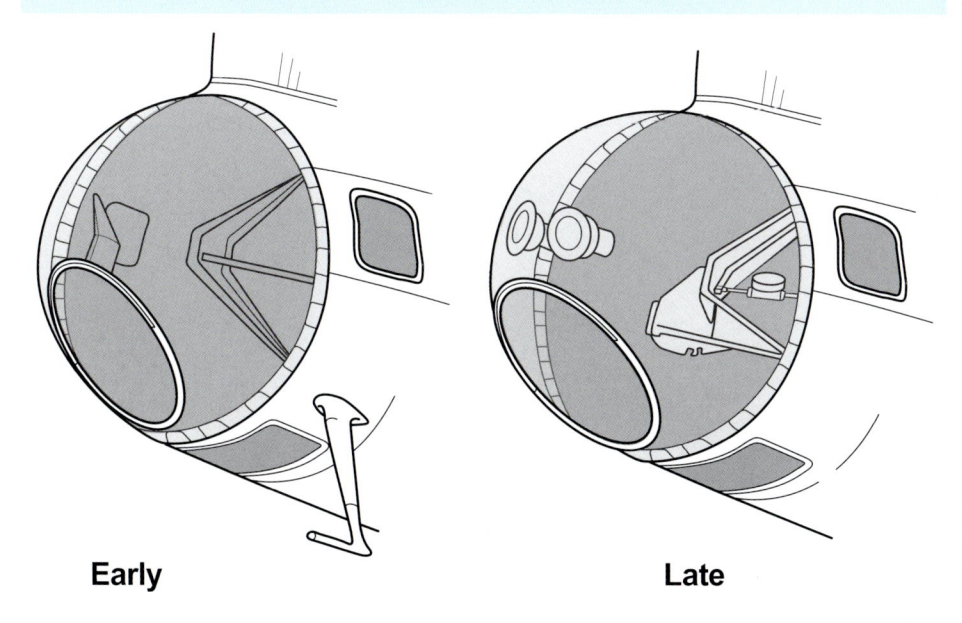

Early

Late

Directly above the bomb aimer's compartment at the front of the aircraft is the KB889's FN5 turret with its two .303 machine-guns. The turret was operated by the bomb aimer but usually only in emergency situations. The small Plexiglas panel ahead of and below the cabin ventilator was a standard fitting.

A close view of the FN5 nose turret shows the thin metal side strips and the heavier frontal frames through which the two .303 machine-guns protrude. The turret base overhangs the fuselage when turret is pointing to the side. The oval shape on top of the turret is a streamlined fairing.

Frazier-Nash 5 Nose Turret

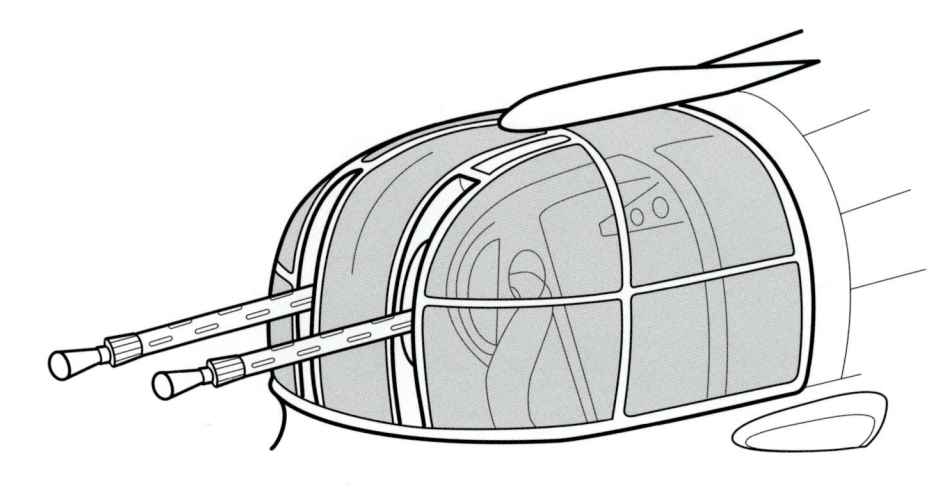

A look at the frontal area on NX611 reveals two variations when compared to KB889. On NX611, the small Plexiglas panel directly behind the bomb aimer's blister is oval, rather than rectangular, in shape. In addition, this Lancaster is equipped with the "H" pattern external aerials for *Rebecca,* the blind-landing equipment. The emblem is that of RAF Bomber Command, whose motto is "Strike Hard, Strike Sure."

Ventilators for the main cockpit area on the Lancaster are positioned on both sides of the fuselage at a point in line with, and below, the end of the FN5 nose turret. The front turret base is oval in shape and slightly overlaps the fuselage side, as seen in this picture.

The trailing aerial fairlead on KB889 is positioned above the portside bomb bay doors and slightly ahead of the leading edge of the wing. On early-production Lancasters this mounting was positioned low down on the starboard fuselage, directly behind the bomb bay rear bulkhead.

The pitot-mast on KB889 is located at the front of the portside longeron and directly below the cockpit windshield. A cloth "sleeve" to prevent dirt entering the tube normally covers the mast. The original position for the pitot-mast on early-production Lancasters was on the same side of the fuselage but directly behind the lower edge of the bomb-aimer's Plexiglas cover.

The oval emergency air charging panel on KB889 is located on the lower port side of the fuselage and several feet behind the trailing aerial fairlead. The words "EMERGENCY AIR CHARGING" are applied in red on the panel, which is held in place by four screws.

Late-production Lancasters such as KB889 were fitted with a large cabin air-filter unit that was positioned on the starboard side of the fuselage. The external cover for the air-filter is shown extending above the rear section of the starboard wing.

The "H2S" blind-navigation and bombing equipment is positioned behind the bomb bay and is housed in a large "teardrop" cover. The main area of cover is sprayed black while its rear section is white. Before "H2S" entered service, early-production Lancasters mounted an FN64 turret in the same location directly behind the bomb bay.

The main entrance door to the Lancaster is located just ahead of the starboard tailplane. The door opens into the fuselage and can be jettisoned in an emergency. Airmen attempting to evacuate the Lancaster by bailing out through this exit ran the risk of striking the horizontal stabilizer.

The external dinghy release cable is positioned above the leading edge of the stabilizer; the operating instruction stencil "DINGHY RELEASE – PULL HERE" is applied in red on this particular Lancaster, NX611. The compartment above which is stencilled "FIRST AID" has been taped over.

A first-aid kit was positioned below and ahead of the starboard horizontal stabilizer of the Lancaster. The container release handle here on Lancaster KB889 is colored red, as are the stenciled words "FIRST AID," which were generally applied directly over the compartment containing a first aid kit on most Lancaster airframes.

Early Mk. I

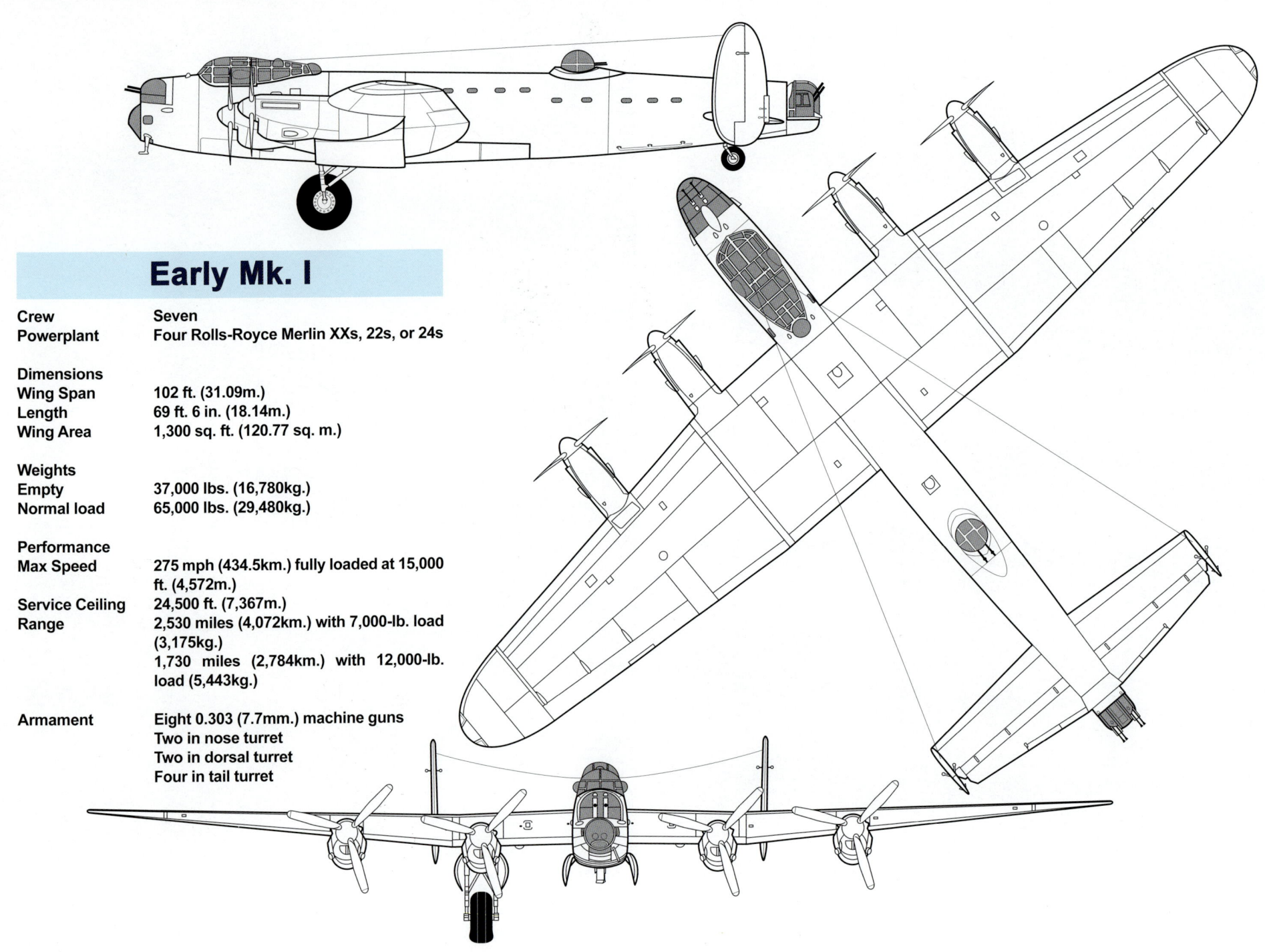

Crew	Seven
Powerplant	Four Rolls-Royce Merlin XXs, 22s, or 24s
Dimensions	
Wing Span	102 ft. (31.09m.)
Length	69 ft. 6 in. (18.14m.)
Wing Area	1,300 sq. ft. (120.77 sq. m.)
Weights	
Empty	37,000 lbs. (16,780kg.)
Normal load	65,000 lbs. (29,480kg.)
Performance	
Max Speed	275 mph (434.5km.) fully loaded at 15,000 ft. (4,572m.)
Service Ceiling	24,500 ft. (7,367m.)
Range	2,530 miles (4,072km.) with 7,000-lb. load (3,175kg.)
	1,730 miles (2,784km.) with 12,000-lb. load (5,443kg.)
Armament	Eight 0.303 (7.7mm.) machine guns
Two in nose turret
Two in dorsal turret
Four in tail turret

Mk. II Lancaster

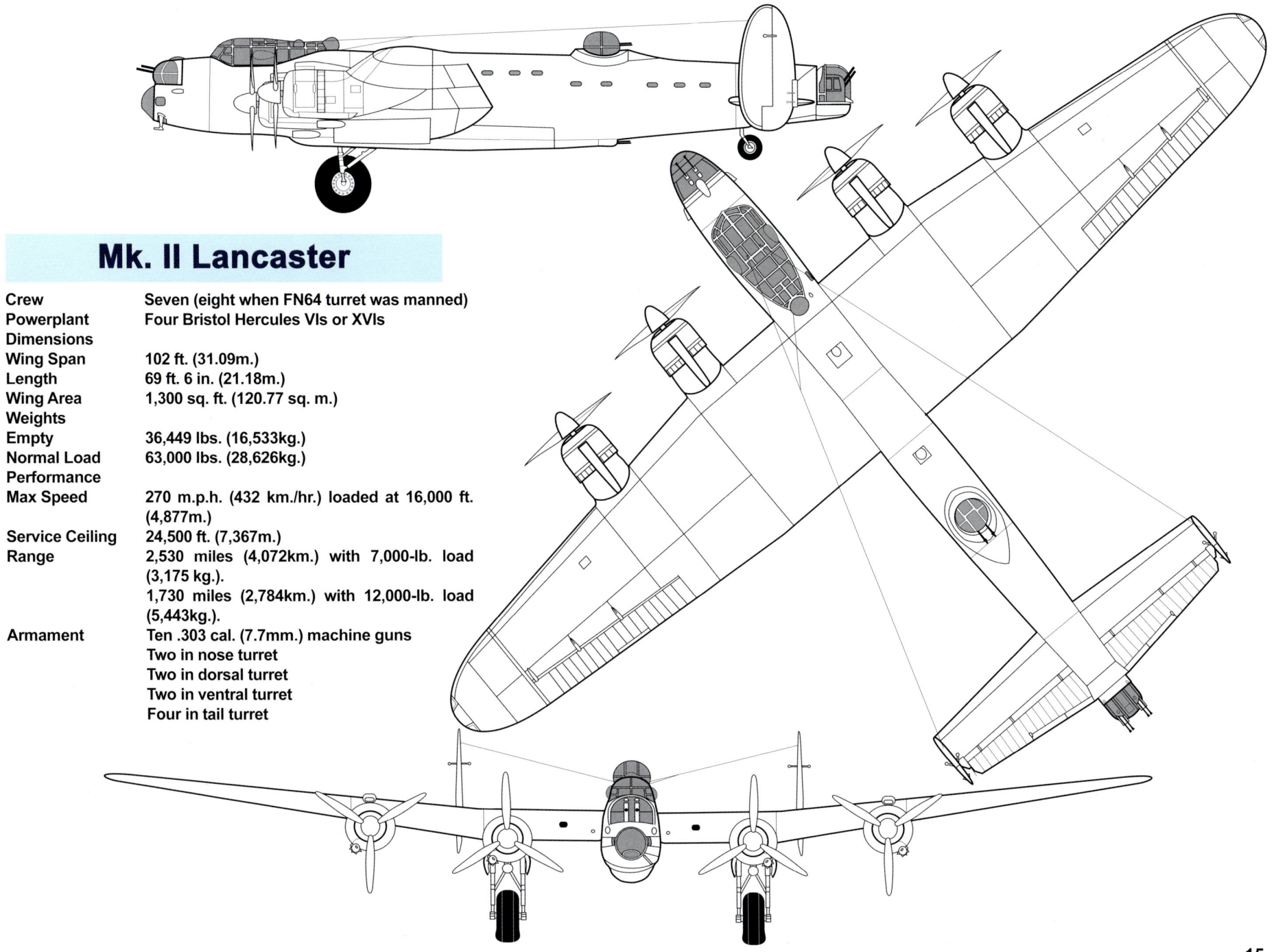

Crew	Seven (eight when FN64 turret was manned)
Powerplant	Four Bristol Hercules VIs or XVIs
Dimensions	
Wing Span	102 ft. (31.09m.)
Length	69 ft. 6 in. (21.18m.)
Wing Area	1,300 sq. ft. (120.77 sq. m.)
Weights	
Empty	36,449 lbs. (16,533kg.)
Normal Load	63,000 lbs. (28,626kg.)
Performance	
Max Speed	270 m.p.h. (432 km./hr.) loaded at 16,000 ft. (4,877m.)
Service Ceiling	24,500 ft. (7,367m.)
Range	2,530 miles (4,072km.) with 7,000-lb. load (3,175 kg.).
	1,730 miles (2,784km.) with 12,000-lb. load (5,443kg.).
Armament	Ten .303 cal. (7.7mm.) machine guns
	Two in nose turret
	Two in dorsal turret
	Two in ventral turret
	Four in tail turret

15

The Lancaster's main defensive firepower is provided by the FN20 rear turret and the FN5 mid-upper turret. Both are hydraulically operated and are equipped with .303 machine guns, which provided a barely adequate counter to the superior firepower of the Luftwaffe night fighters.

Frazer-Nash 20 Tail Turret

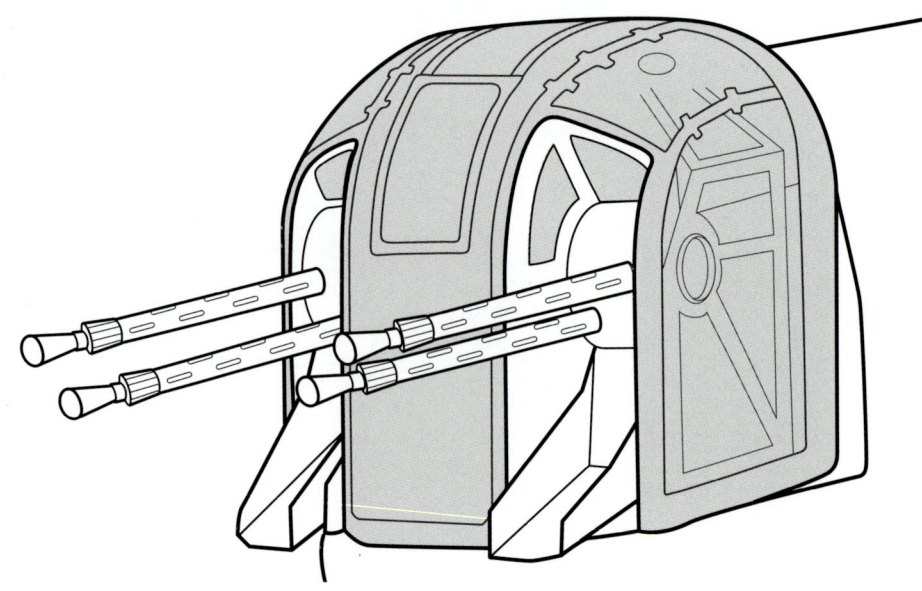

This is the FN20 rear turret on KB889. The turret was operated by an engine-driven pump mounted in the port (left) outer engine. The gunner's vision panel in the center of the turret is complete in this case. The Plexiglas was often totally removed, however, in order to provide the gunner with clear visibility. The temperature drop suffered by the already frozen gunner as a result was no more than a few degrees.

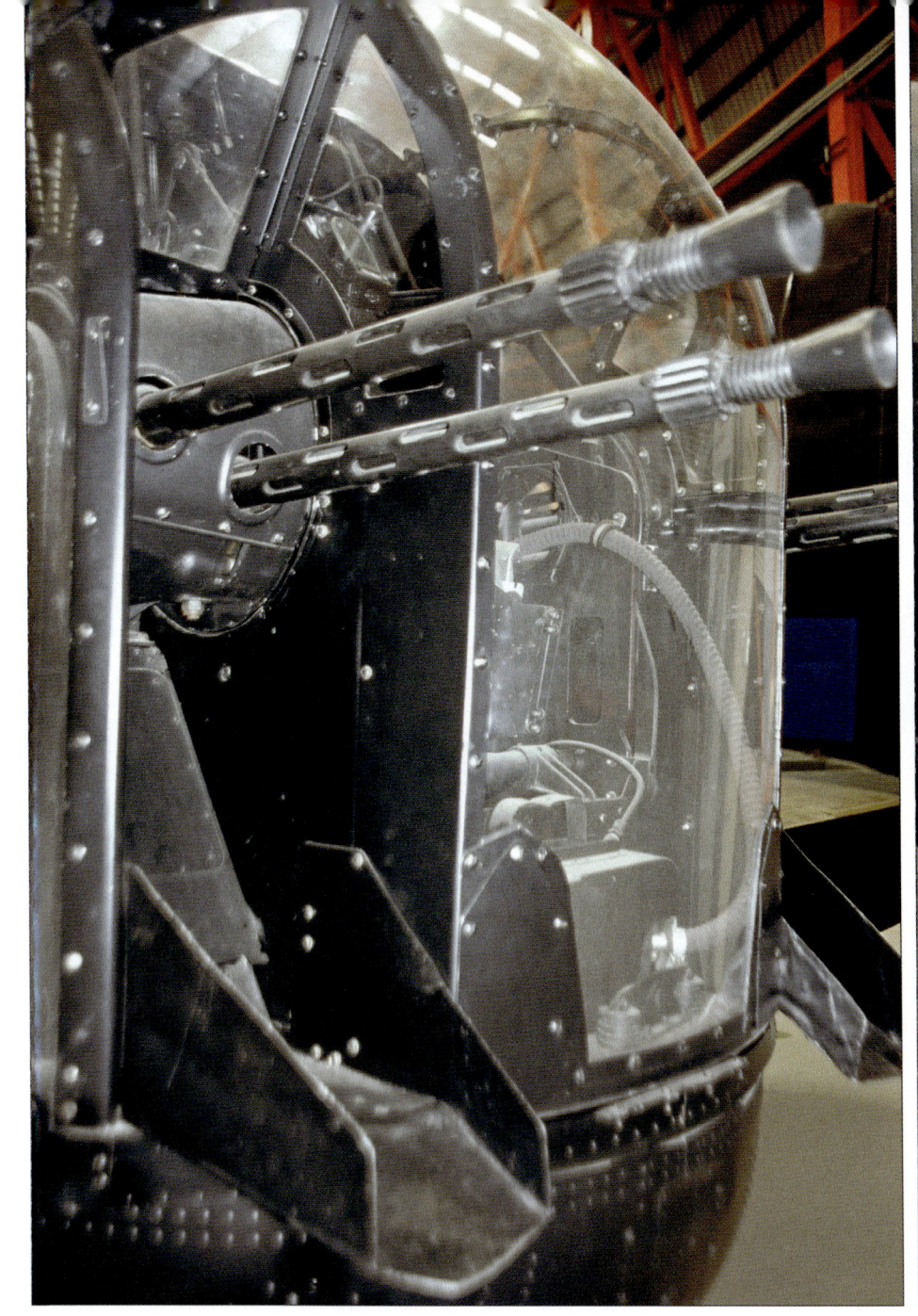

Extending from the curved mounting frame is the right-side pair of machine guns on KB889's rear turret (on the aircraft's port side). Cooling sleeves with rectangular vents enclose each barrel. Large cartridge ejection chutes are fitted to the base of the turret.

The Lancaster's extreme rear fuselage is flared out at a slight angle where it matches up with the rear turret. This design allows for the free movement of the turret when it is being operated. The outside of the turret is colored black, overall

This inside view of the FN20 rear turret shows the black vertical support for the gun operating hand grips, which angle downward from the top of the support. Green padding covers the gunner's seat, which has no back support.

Machine gun charging handles on the left-side weapons are colored white. The inner guns are set at a lower level than the outer weapons. The angled-back support strut for the left-center vertical frame of the turret is black and is seen in foreground.

The FN20 four-gun turret was replaced on late-production Lancasters by the FN82. The number of weapons was reduced to two but these were of the heavier .50 caliber type. The example seen here is fitted to NX611. The external profile of the turret is basically similar to its FN20 predecessor.

The internal layout of the FN82 turret features a chain-drive mechanism fitted to the side of each weapon. The gunner also seems to have a more generous area in which to function in the FN82 turret than in the FN20.

The Lancaster rear turret was fitted with a pair of sliding metal doors, like these seen on KB889's FN20 turret. On the left side is a circular Plexiglas panel with an external handgrip below it.

Mounted in the NX611's FN82 rear turret are .50 caliber machine guns. The top of the FN82 turret frame is flatter than that of the FN20. The FN82's shell-ejection chutes are also wider to accommodate the .50 caliber shell casings that were longer than the .303.

The gunner's hand grips, used in firing the .50 caliber machine guns, are mounted on a column inside the FN82 rear turret. Above the grips is the turret gun-sight with a switch used to determine the wingspan of aircraft attacking the Lancaster.

The FN50 mid-upper turret provides a good sighting platform for the gunner. The raised shape surrounding the turret base contains a tracking system that is designed to prevent the machine guns from firing into the aircraft's own structure.

The Martin mid-upper turret fitted to KB889 has two .50 caliber machine-guns. These weapons had a greater striking power than the standard .303 guns mounted in the majority of British-built turrets during WWII. The frameless Plexiglas cover also provided a superb field of all-round vision for the gunner.

The cooling jackets on the .303 machine guns are visible in this view of the FN50 mid-upper turret on PA474. The portside metal arm with colored circular end is attached to the turret frame and keeps the gun barrel from dropping below the horizontal angle.

The Martin turret has a lower profile than the standard FN50 turret frame, and cannot be fitted with the guardrails that keep the guns from inadvertently firing into the Lancaster's airframe. Raised metal strips are positioned on the upper fuselage on either side of the Martin turret, and are part of the strengthening frame around the turret base.

The codes on PA474 relate to a No. 103 Sqdn. aircraft that amassed a record total of 141 operations (missions) within Bomber Command. It was also nicknamed "M-squared" or "Mother of them all." The 2 denotes a second Sqdn. aircraft bearing the letter M.

Unfaired Dorsal Turret

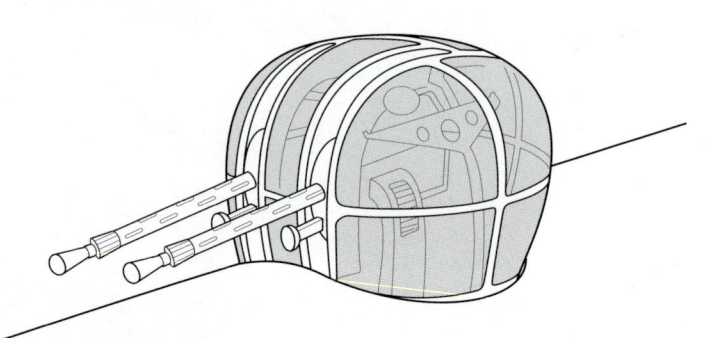

Faired Dorsal Turret

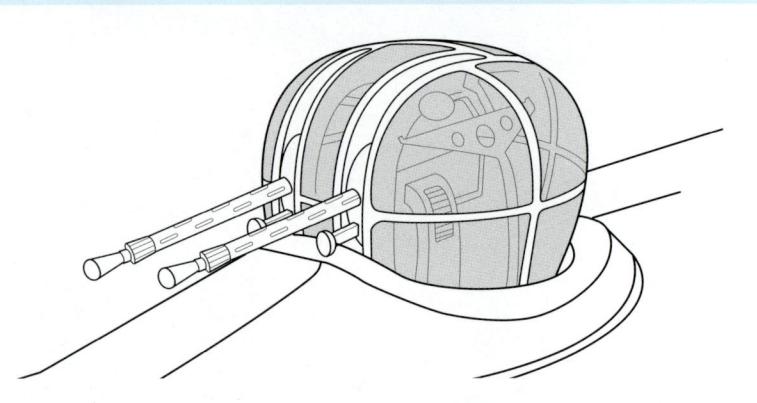

The Lancaster's fin and rudder on PA484 display the standard oval shape as fitted to the Avro bomber. The overall black color on the fin and rudder surfaces was normally only broken by the inclusion of the fin flash.

The separation line between the fin and rudder on NX611 and the three rudder hinges are clearly visible. Circular panels below the fin flash access the stabilizer/rudder linking bolts, while the panel on the left also accesses the rudder trim-tab mechanism.

Tail Development

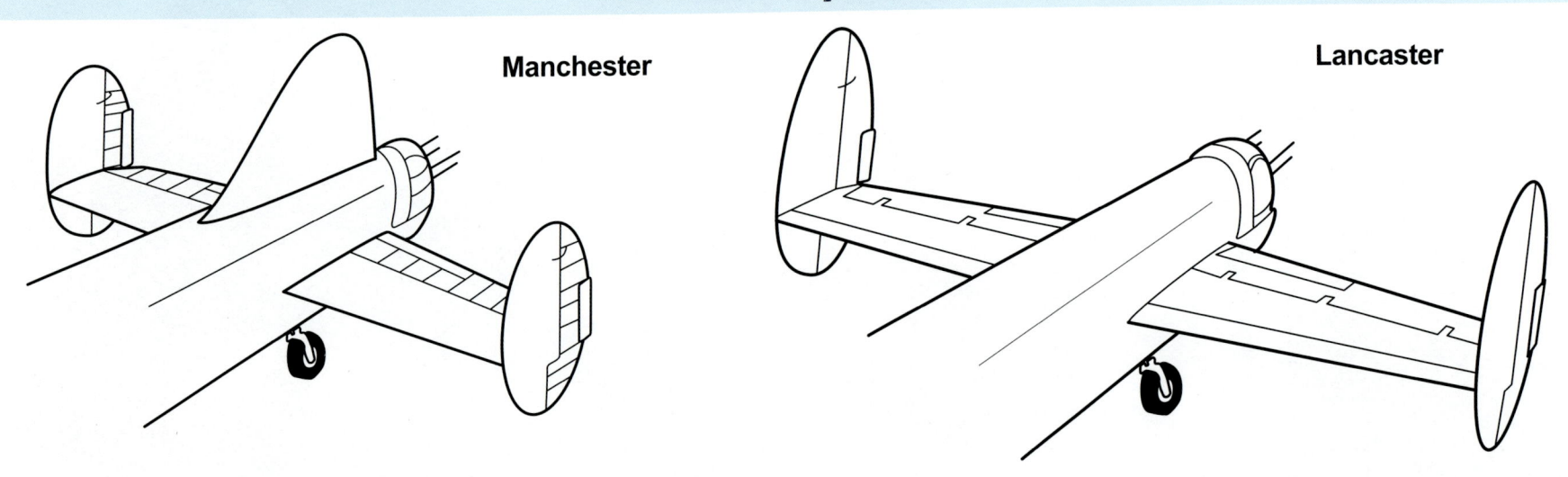

Manchester

Lancaster

A close-up view of the port-inner rudder mass balance weight on KB889 shows how it is secured in place by recessed screws. An aerial wire with its tension-adjuster is seen directly above the mass balance "teardrop" cover.

The rudder trim-tabs on KB889 are fitted with standard mass balance weights positioned in the center of the tab. Also shown is the tab control rod slotting into the rudder surface.

The rudder trim-tabs on NX611 are the standard pattern for the Lancaster. However, there are no mass balance weights fitted. Detachable panels give access to the trim-tab controls.

The Lancaster stabilizers have a total span of 33 ft. They are positioned just below the center-line of the rear fuselage and ahead of the rear turret. Four large bolts hold the pair of stabilizers together inside the fuselage.

The starboard elevator on NX611 is seen here in a slightly lowered position. The balance tab in the center of the elevator moves automatically in a counter-direction to the elevator.

Three hinges attach the elevator to the stabilizer, as seen in this overhead view of the starboard elevator and stabilizer on KB8889. Both stabilizer and elevator surfaces are metal covered, but early- and mid-production Lancasters had fabric-covered elevators.

The Lancaster elevators are fitted with pairs of trim tabs. This is one of the inner tabs, which are manually adjusted by the pilot, using a large wheel positioned on the cockpit floor alongside the right side of his seat.

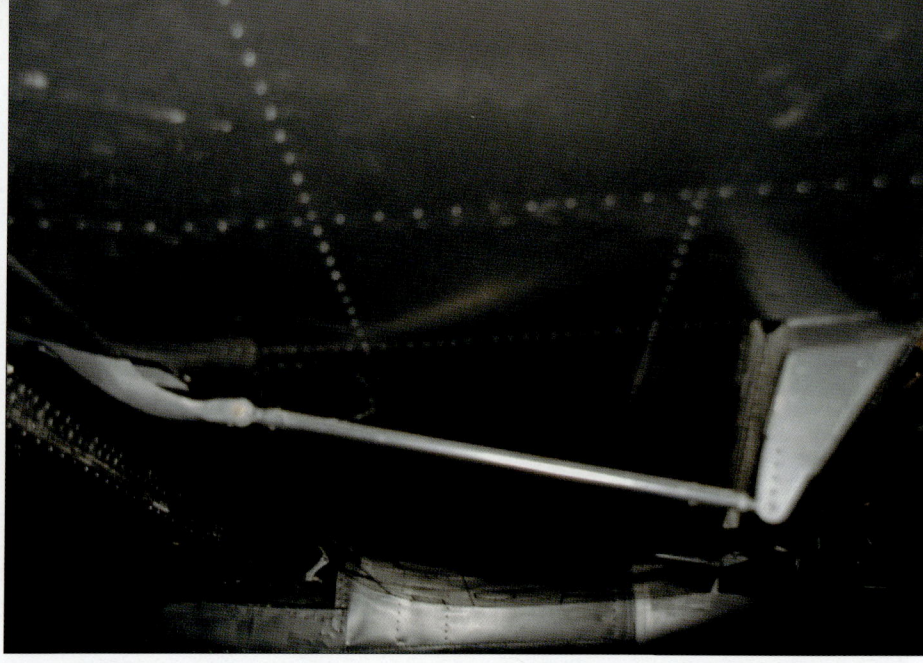

The outer tabs on the Lancaster's elevators operate on a "balance" action; when the elevator is raised or lowered, the tab automatically compensates by moving in the opposite direction.

The connecting rod for the left side elevator balance tab on KB889 is fitted to the outer edge of the tab and links up with the elevator hinge bracket.

The Lancaster's tail wheel shock absorber slots into a circular aperture that is part of a rectangular box frame. The red line extending across the fuselage indicates where to place the rear trestle when raising the aircraft off its landing gear.

Tail Wheel

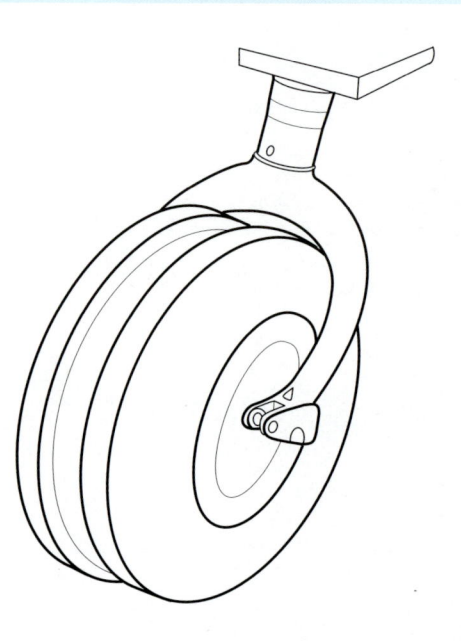

The Lancaster's tail wheel is non-retractable but moves through 360 degrees. The wheel hub is mounted in an "inverted U" bracket. The distinctive tire shape with raised outer edges is intended to prevent the wheel from "shimmying" during landing and take-off.

This side view of the Lancaster's tail wheel shows the angle of the "inverted U" support bracket and the shock absorber attachment extending up into the fuselage. The support bracket is black and the shock absorber is finished in natural metal.

The Lancaster's wings span 102 ft. and are positioned above the bomb bay. Each wing consists of three sections. The inner section extends to a point just outside the inner engine mounts. The center section finishes at the outer edge of the aileron, where it links up with the wing-tip section.

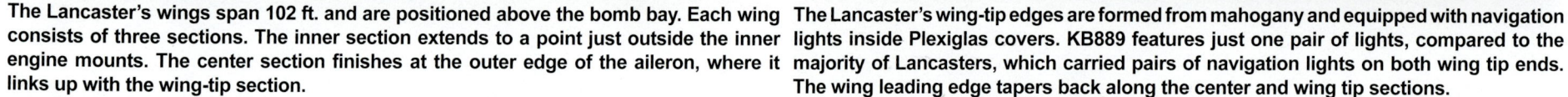

The Lancaster's ailerons are 17 ft. long and extend from a point directly behind the outer engine nacelles to match up with the wing tip sections. The frame consists of a single spar supporting 21 ribs. The aileron frames were covered with fabric on early Lancasters. Later-production batches featured metal-covered ailerons.

The Lancaster's wing-tip edges are formed from mahogany and equipped with navigation lights inside Plexiglas covers. KB889 features just one pair of lights, compared to the majority of Lancasters, which carried pairs of navigation lights on both wing tip ends. The wing leading edge tapers back along the center and wing tip sections.

The starboard balance tab on KB889 is operated by a strut linked to the inner aileron hinge bracket. The rear end of the balance control rod is attached to a vertical bracket positioned in the center of the tab. Only the starboard aileron on Mk. I Lancasters featured two tabs, the port aileron being fitted with the balance tab only.

28

The single black line seen here runs along the breadth of each inner wing section on the Lancaster. There is a second single line running just ahead of the dinghy hatch. Wording WALK AFT OF THIS LINE is also in black. (Wording applied ahead of the rear line says WALK FORWARD OF THIS LINE).

The square panel outline directly behind the black walkway line on NX611 covers the standard dinghy stowage container. The Plexiglas inspection plate is seen in the bottom left-hand corner of the panel

The inner trim-tab on the Lancaster's starboard aileron is controlled by the pilot, using a knurled wheel situated between the pilot's seat and the elevator trim-tab wheel. The rectangular panel is a detachable cover over the aileron control arm.

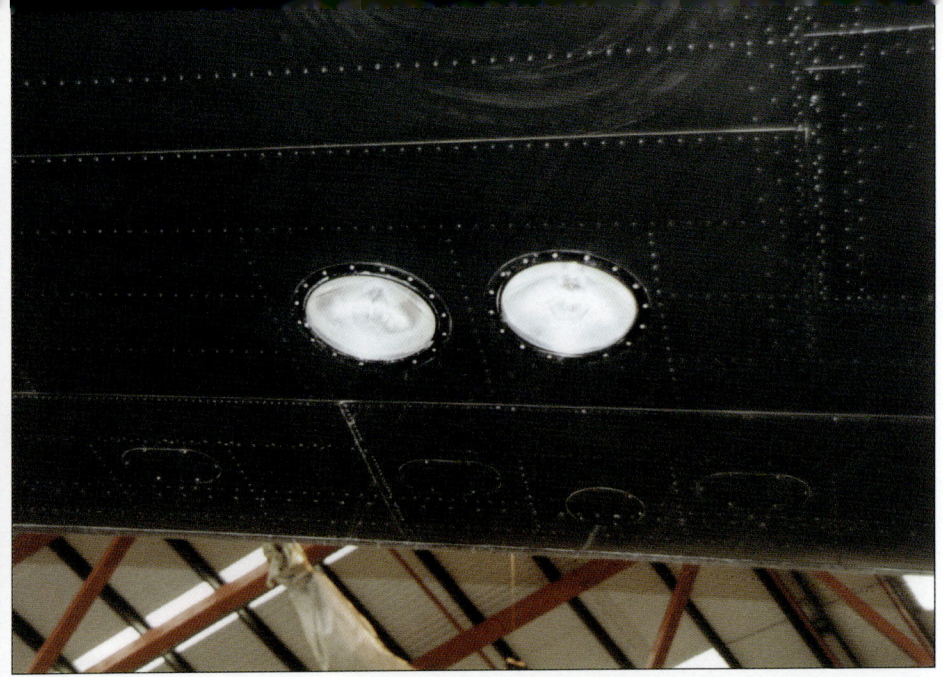

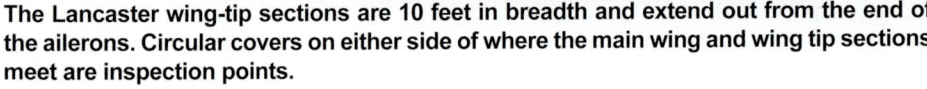

The Lancaster wing-tip sections are 10 feet in breadth and extend out from the end of the ailerons. Circular covers on either side of where the main wing and wing tip sections meet are inspection points.

Parallel lines running fore and aft under the Lancaster's outer wings indicate where the outer trestles are to be positioned when the aircraft is raised off its landing gear. Lines and words TRESTLE HERE are applied in red.

The Lancaster's landing lights are positioned under the left wing, between the wing spars and in line with the outer aileron hinge. The Plexiglas covers are fixed in position and the lights are angled downwards to provide the necessary light-beam direction.

The Lancaster's wings have four mooring points to secure the aircraft to the ground. They are located at the leading edges of the wing, between the engines and slightly inboard from the junction with the wing-tip seams.

Pitot Mast

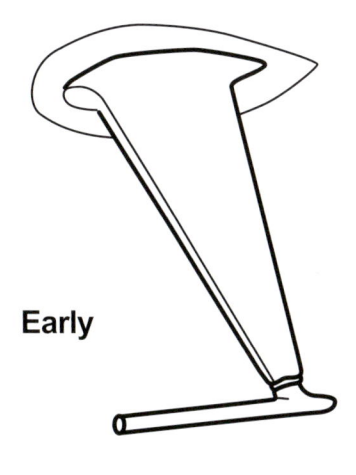

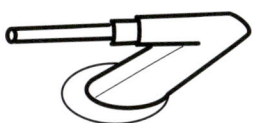

Early

Late

Two large scoops are located under the leading edges of the wing next to the fuselage. These are part of the Lancaster's hot/cold air system. The interior of the scoop appears to be sprayed interior green.

Each Merlin engine is equipped with a fuel booster pump. The pumps are located under the wings – on either side of the inboard engines and outside the outer pair of engines. "Teardrop-shaped" covers are fitted over all six pumps. The panel on the left accesses the equipment used for emergency dumping of the fuel tanks, but only from the two inner tanks.

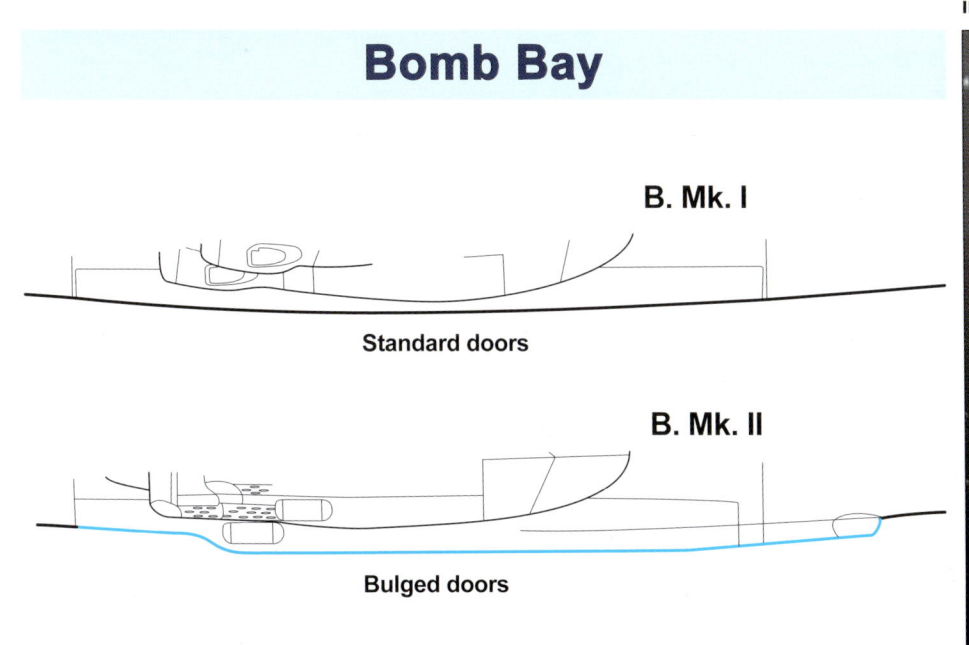

Bomb Bay

B. Mk. I

Standard doors

B. Mk. II

Bulged doors

There are two flaps on the Lancaster's wings that extend out between the fuselage and the ailerons. This is the inner flap unit that spans the breadth of the inner wing section. The flap surface is sprayed interior green

This is one of the outer wing flaps on NX611. The thin struts at the top of the flap are linked to the flap-operating rod. The flap edging-strip contains a row of lightening holes. The separation line between the two flap sections is clearly seen here.

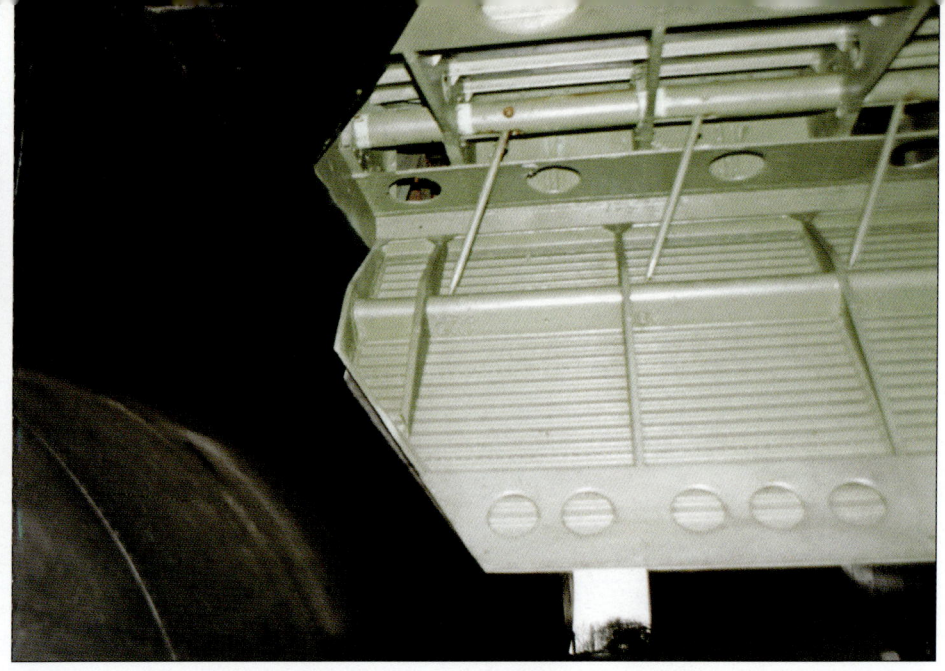

The rear section of the inside flap's inner edge is angled outwards in order to clear the bomb bay doors when these are in the open position.

The detachable port-inner fuel tank on PA474 (not present here) would fit in this position. It normally contained 580 imperial gallons. The four steel restraining straps are tan in color. Two further tanks in each wing hold 497 additional imperial gallons, providing a maximum capacity of 2,154 imperial gallons.

The Lancaster's landing gear units consist of two vertical struts on either side of the wheel. The struts extend up into the front of the wheel bay and are attached to angled-back frames mounted on the main wing spar and angle-mounted rods extending into the engine firewall.

Two "inverted V" bracing struts are located between the main landing gear struts, as seen in this frontal view of the Lancaster landing gear. Each bracing strut is attached to a main strut level with the top of the wheel. They join up at a point just above the bottom of the engine nacelle.

Mk. VII Lancaster

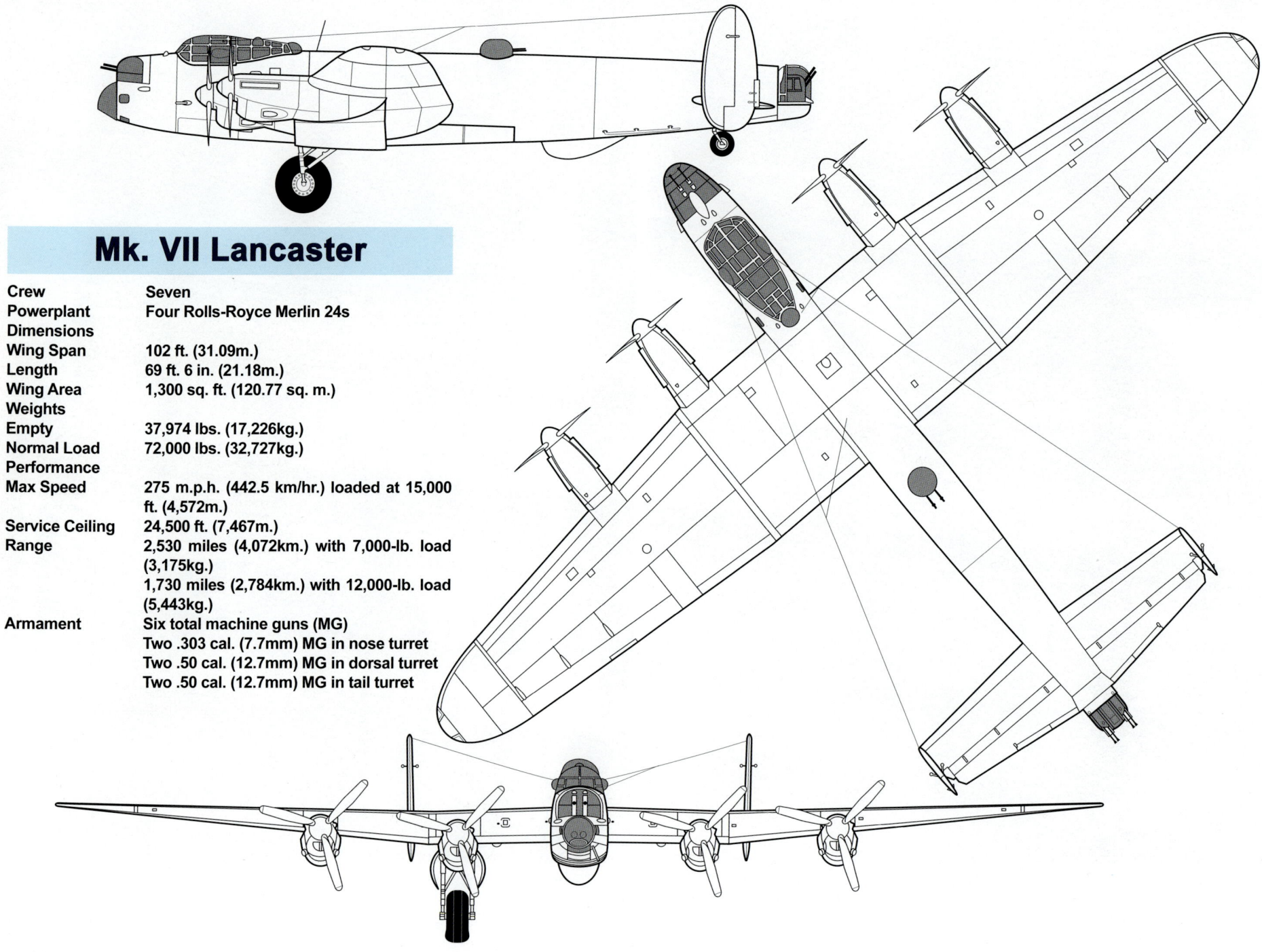

Crew	Seven
Powerplant	Four Rolls-Royce Merlin 24s
Dimensions	
Wing Span	102 ft. (31.09m.)
Length	69 ft. 6 in. (21.18m.)
Wing Area	1,300 sq. ft. (120.77 sq. m.)
Weights	
Empty	37,974 lbs. (17,226kg.)
Normal Load	72,000 lbs. (32,727kg.)
Performance	
Max Speed	275 m.p.h. (442.5 km/hr.) loaded at 15,000 ft. (4,572m.)
Service Ceiling	24,500 ft. (7,467m.)
Range	2,530 miles (4,072km.) with 7,000-lb. load (3,175kg.)
	1,730 miles (2,784km.) with 12,000-lb. load (5,443kg.)
Armament	Six total machine guns (MG)
	Two .303 cal. (7.7mm) MG in nose turret
	Two .50 cal. (12.7mm) MG in dorsal turret
	Two .50 cal. (12.7mm) MG in tail turret

34

The main landing gear struts are finished in natural metal apart from the center section, which is black. A black colored strut extending from the rear of the main strut to the landing gear door cover ensures that the door automatically closes when the landing gear is retracted.

The Lancaster's landing gear retracts backwards into the engine nacelle. The white colored "break-point" contains the locking mechanism for the main landing gear radius rod. The red colored strut is not part of the landing gear, but acts as an extra support for KB889 while it is on exhibition at the IWM Museum, Duxford.

The main landing gear radius rod (below) and the jack piston rod (above) are linked to the "break-point." The jack piston rod is a telescopic unit. Both rods are attached to the rear wall of the engine nacelle and fold upwards into the nacelle when the gear is retracted.

This view of the right side radius and jack piston rods shows how the upper rod is linked directly above the "break-point" to a horizontal bracing strut and an angled bracing strut. The angled strut extends upwards from the horizontal strut and has a "U"-pattern end piece linking it to the jack piston rod. The wing rib design is seen at the top of the photograph.

In this forward internal view of the Lancaster's engine nacelle, the two red bottles positioned in the nacelle roof behind the firewall are fire extinguishers. Bracing struts in the foreground are attached to the upper radius rod. The light-colored frames in the center of the picture link the landing gear struts to the main wing spar.

The tire on NX611 shows the distinctive tread pattern used by the Dunlop Company on these late-production examples. Pieces of cloth have been placed on the top of the tire to prevent oil-drippings from adversely affecting the tire surface. Fully-fitted covers were placed over the Lancaster's main wheels as an anti-oil precaution during WWII.

The Lancaster landing gear wheels are nearly six feet in diameter. The "U"-shaped frame attached to the base of the main strut is repeated on the other side, with both acting as towing points. The tire brake line loops up behind the main strut. The original tires used on the Lancaster had no tread pattern.

The Merlin engine is fitted with a large air scoop positioned under the propeller spinner. Air is channelled to the oil and coolant radiators located just inside the scoop.

The Merlin engines on Lancasters came from two national production sources. The original source was Rolls-Royce in Britain but a licence was later granted the U.S. Packard Company to build Merlins. The sole difference between a Mk. I Lancaster and the Mk. III and X was that the Mk. I used engines from the Rolls-Royce factories. The engines in this picture are mounted on the Duxford Museum's Mk. X/KB889.

The Lancaster's hydromatic propellers fitted to the Merlin engine are produced by the American company Hamilton. They are of metal construction and are fitted with constant-speed units. The yellow tips to the blades provide a necessary visual guide to personnel, standing near an aircraft under power, helping them to keep clear of the spinning propellers.

The removal of the cowling panels from PA474's No. 1 engine reveals the main engine bearer frame, which is sprayed in interior green. Also exposed is the engine radiator, with its silver finished outer cover and semi-hexagonal shape. The engine oil tank is finished in orange. Inspection panels under the outer wing surface have been removed.

Small "foot-steps" are attached directly below the "break-point" on the main radius rods. These enable the ground crew to gain access to the inner nacelle and plug in the auxiliary starter battery cable. This was a difficult duty, especially when wearing clumsy boots and working in wet or frosty weather conditions.

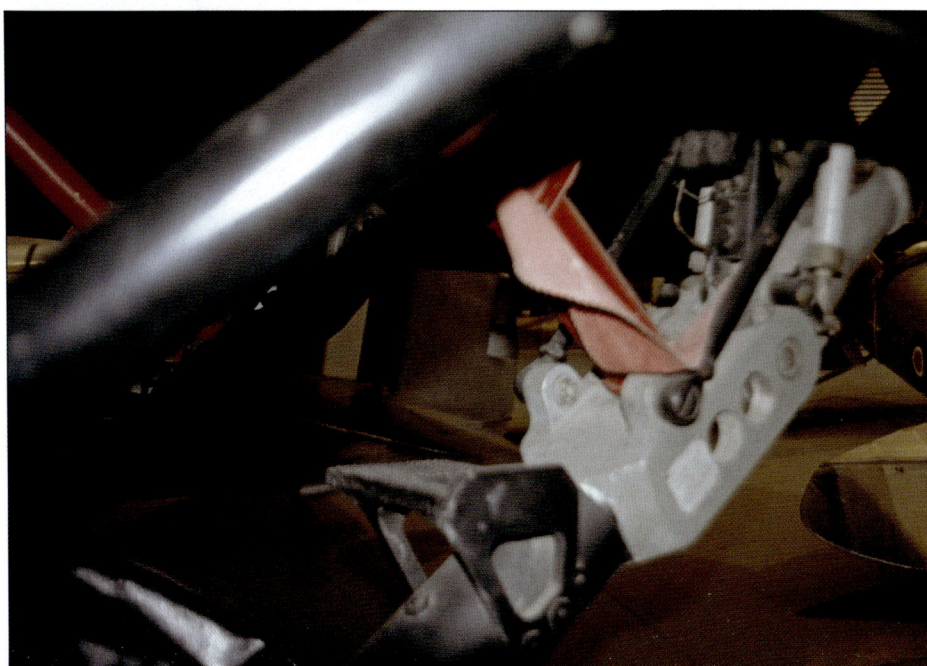

The No. 1 engine on KB889 is stripped of its cowling. The silver glycol tank is directly behind the propeller base-plate with the filler cap positioned towards the top. The main engine block is black with silver plug-leads. The engine firewall is sprayed interior green. The wing section behind the No. 2 engine is raised to permit maintenance.

This close-up of the Merlin exhaust stacks shows how each one is formed of two sections welded together. The scoop below and ahead of the forward stack channels cool air onto the spark plugs. Exhaust stacks and scoops would have been covered by a flame-damping shroud during WWII.

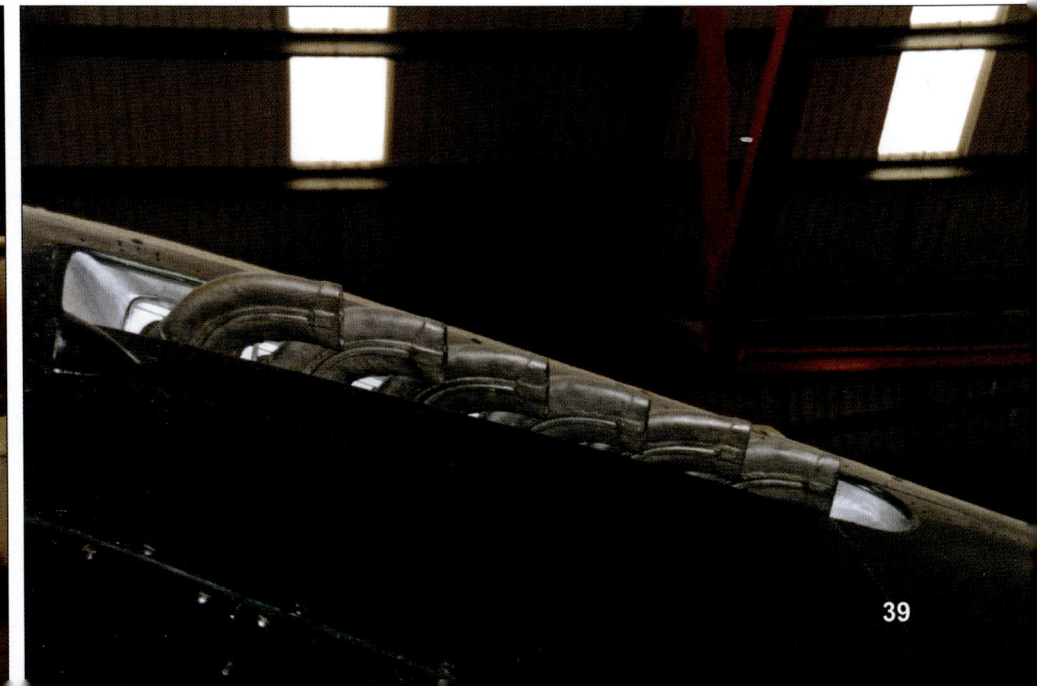

The starboard flap on NX611 is in the lowered position. This picture shows how the rear section of the engine nacelle, which is attached to the inner flap surface, folds into the main nacelle compartment.

The Lancaster's inboard engine nacelles extend back to the wing trailing edges. Visible here is the separation line for the flexible rear sections, which are attached to the flaps and move back into the main nacelles when the flaps are operated.

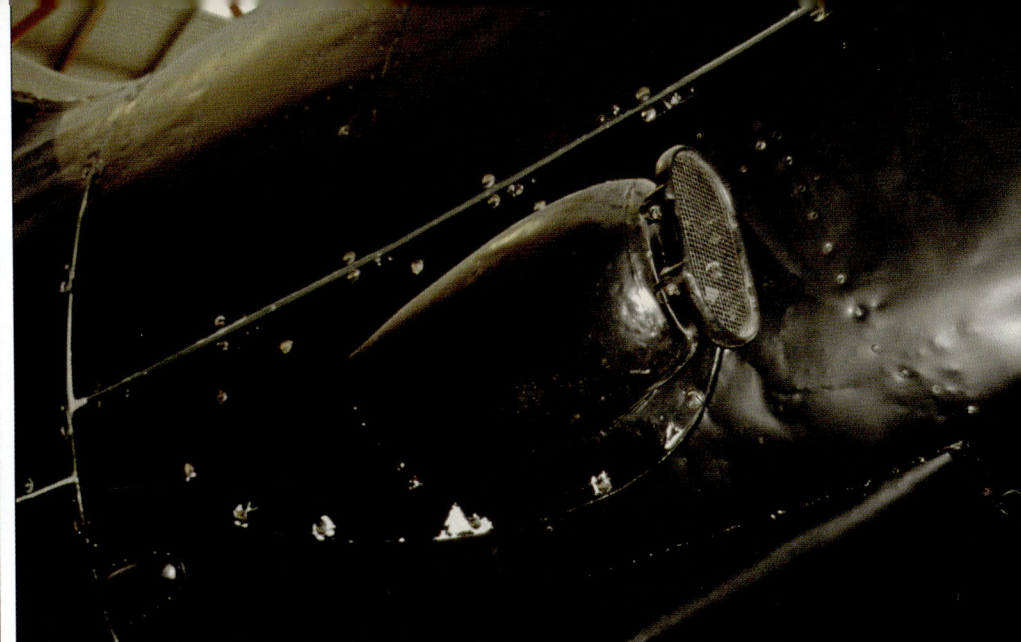

The coolant and oil radiator shutter control cover on this Merlin engine cowling is in the lowered position. The panel directly behind the shutter cover gives access when opened to the engine carburetor.

A panel on the starboard-outer Merlin cowling's right-side, which is positioned directly below the wing's leading edge, provides access to the water collection trap that services the Lancaster's various pneumatic systems. The instruction to drain the trap daily is applied in red.

The Merlin engines are fitted with carburetor air intakes, which are located on both sides of the cowling. Oval-shaped mesh screens are mounted on the front of the intakes in order to prevent the carburetors icing-up or being adversely affected by dust or dirt.

The left side cowling panels on the Merlins that are directly under the wing leading edges provide access to the engine oil tanks. The tanks are self-sealing and hold 37½ imperial gallons with a further 4½ imperial gallons of air space. Stack-pipes in the tanks retain ⅔ imperial gallon for possible use in "feathering" the propellers.

Space in the bomb aimer's compartment is very restricted. Immediately to the aimer's left is the analogue computer unit that measures the various factors (wind-speed, drift, etc.) necessary for making accurate use of the Mk. XIV bombsight. The gyros inside the computer unit are operated by a vacuum pump fitted to the port-inner engine. The box cover is sprayed overall black with operating instructions in white.

A forward view of the bomb aimer's compartment shows the circular shape of the optical flat through which the bombsight is focused. Two circular metal shapes above the optical flat are infrared sensors whose signal acted as a "friendly" indicator to Lancasters equipped with Automatic Gun-Laying Turret (AGLT) rear gun turrets.

The Mk. XIV bombsight is seen in position on board PA474. The bombsight support platform is positioned directly behind the optical flat and extends over the downward-vision Plexiglas panel at the base of the fuselage. The support is painted black along with the rest of the bomb aimer's compartment.

The bomb-aimer's operating panel is positioned on the forward-starboard side of the nose compartment, and is sprayed in overall black. Two rows of switches at the top left of the panel are the bomb selector switches. Directly below them is the apparatus for controlling "stick-bombing," with the gray dial at the bottom determining the interval between each bomb's release. The selector box in the center-bottom of the panel determined the order of dropping the bombs in order to keep the bomber correctly stabilized. The bomb-release cable is coiled around the selector box.

The Lancaster's camera is located on the port rear side of the nose compartment. It is mounted on a gray rectangular frame and focused vertically through a circular Plexiglas panel. Its operation was linked to the release of a photo-flare that provided the necessary exposure light.

Entry to the bomb-aimer's compartment is to the right of the main cockpit area. Yellow-sprayed frames provide necessary handgrips for moving through this very confined space. The bomb aimer's operating panel is visible in the background.

The two instruments fitted in the center of KB889's windshield are the distant reading (D.R.) compass repeater (top) and the direction finder (D.F.) indicator (bottom). The D.F. indicator was sometimes positioned separately to the immediate left of the windshield's central frame, with the D.R. compass repeater lowered to the top of the instrument panel. The handgrip mounted on the left upper cockpit frame is wrapped in white material.

The forward vertical cockpit panels slide forward and back and are operated by the horizontal rods seen here. The clear-vision panel at the top right of the picture opens inward and is operated by using the small gray knurled wheel at the base of the panel.

The main engine control quadrant on KB889 is painted silver. The four engine throttle levers are on the top; these are silver with black knobs, the outer pair being angled inwards. The four silver levers in the lower section of the quadrant control the propeller revolutions. Master fuel cock levers are mounted in pairs on the two silver-colored panels at the base of the instrument panel, which is painted black overall.

Two rows of dials directly ahead of the throttle quadrant monitor the engine boost (top row) and RPMs performance (bottom row). The small panel below the right-side pair of RPM gauges is the supercharger gear control-change.

The port side of the pilot's main instrument panel contains the standard instrument dials for use in blind-flying conditions. The dial in the top center of the panel is perhaps the most vital; it is the artificial horizon. Directly below the artificial horizon is the direction indicator. The two dials to the left of the blind-flying panel are (top) the beam approach indicator and (bottom) the landing gear position indicator.

The horizontal row of four large, red pushbuttons operates the propeller "feathering" mechanisms. The second row of pushbuttons at the base of the instrument panel is for operating the engine fire extinguishers. The black vacuum changeover cock lever is in the center of the picture, and the signalling switchbox controlling the identification lamps is at the bottom right of the instrument panel.

The pilot was provided with an armored panel for protection of his upper body. It was attached to the top of the seat frame by two arms and hinged at the bottom, which allowed the panel to be folded back down behind the seat. The panel was distinguished by the yellow circle, and was the sole piece of armor on a Lancaster. The seat padding is covered in dark green leather. The knurled, silver wheel is the rudder trim-tab control.

The Lancaster's P4 compass is positioned down on the port side and ahead of the pilot's seat. The empty dial frame directly below the compass normally houses the auto controls pressure gauge. The dial above the compass relates to the operation of the flaps. The inverted "L" rod sprayed red is part of the control column locking mechanism and is secured permanently to the airframe.

Grand Slam

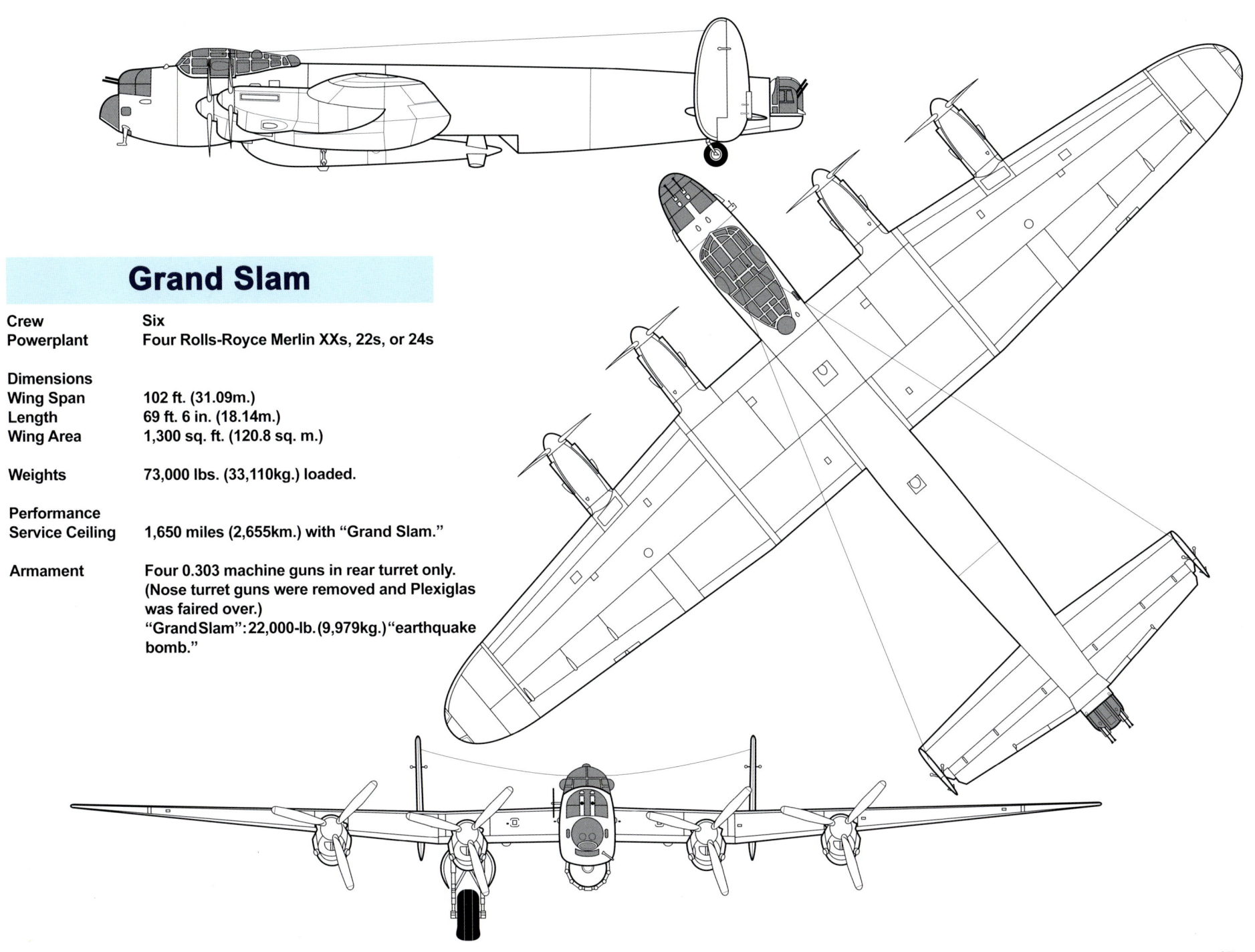

Crew	Six
Powerplant	Four Rolls-Royce Merlin XXs, 22s, or 24s
Dimensions	
Wing Span	102 ft. (31.09m.)
Length	69 ft. 6 in. (18.14m.)
Wing Area	1,300 sq. ft. (120.8 sq. m.)
Weights	73,000 lbs. (33,110kg.) loaded.
Performance	
Service Ceiling	1,650 miles (2,655km.) with "Grand Slam."
Armament	Four 0.303 machine guns in rear turret only. (Nose turret guns were removed and Plexiglas was faired over.) "Grand Slam": 22,000-lb. (9,979kg.) "earthquake bomb."

The standard Lancaster handgrip for the pilot consists of a "U"-shaped design with a "Y" pattern structure mounted between the hand-grip itself and acting as a bracing device. The handgrip is attached to the top of a large rectangular control column. A curved brake lever is attached to the left side of the "Y" frame. The red, inverted-"L" control locking rod is a modern item.

The head armor on PA474 is photographed in the fold-down position while the right armrest is swung up to allow the pilot access to the seat. The dark red wheel at the base of the seat frame controls the trim of the ailerons. The net container at bottom right of the seat frame normally holds oxygen bottles. The red frame locks the landing gear lever in place and is a modern item.

48

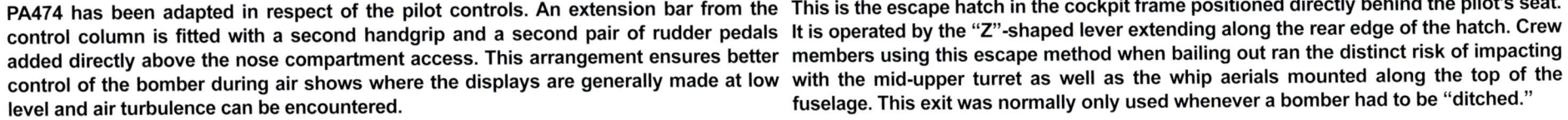

PA474 has been adapted in respect of the pilot controls. An extension bar from the control column is fitted with a second handgrip and a second pair of rudder pedals added directly above the nose compartment access. This arrangement ensures better control of the bomber during air shows where the displays are generally made at low level and air turbulence can be encountered.

This is the escape hatch in the cockpit frame positioned directly behind the pilot's seat. It is operated by the "Z"-shaped lever extending along the rear edge of the hatch. Crew members using this escape method when bailing out ran the distinct risk of impacting with the mid-upper turret as well as the whip aerials mounted along the top of the fuselage. This exit was normally only used whenever a bomber had to be "ditched."

The direction-finding loop can be seen in the foreground in this view of the rear section of the cockpit frame, which extends several feet back beyond the rear edge of the pilot's cockpit section. The interior framing of the cockpit is painted black.

The "teardrop" Plexiglas "bulge" on KB889's cockpit frame is positioned directly above the Flight Engineer's panel. Some production batches repeated the "bulge" on the port-side of the cockpit as seen on PA474.

49

The Flight Engineer's collapsible seat is seen in position. The dark green seat cover in its black metal base swings over and its left side rests on a tubular frame attached to the pilot's seat frame. A movable black-sprayed bar linked to the metal support directly behind the backrest keeps this section of the seat arrangement in place.

The main control panels for the flight engineer are positioned on the right side of the fuselage directly behind the pilot's seat. The engineer's primary duty was to monitor the fuel consumption and to transfer fuel from tank to tank as required. The fuel tank selector cocks are positioned center-left on the larger panel with the electric fuel booster pump switches directly above.

Directly behind the semi-bulkhead, to which the navigator's table is attached, is the wireless operator's table in KB889. On it are a TR1154 transmitter and TR1155 receiver.

The repeater panel at top right of this shot of the navigator's section has dials for airspeed and altitude. The D/F loop control switch is mounted inside the silver frame at top left. The desk is also equipped with an angle-poise lamp. The blue curtain on extreme right was drawn across fuselage to cut off all external light from the navigator's position.

The wireless operator's position in PA474 features a more updated wartime layout than it does in KB889. The Morse-key is located on the right of the desk. The piece of equipment on the left side of the desk is a "fishpond" set, which warned of aircraft approaching from behind.

The navigator's table is positioned along the left side of the interior and runs back to the bulkhead frame. The frame formed the back edge of what was the second separate fuselage section. The blue curtain on the right would be pulled across to ensure that the desk lighting would not be seen from outside.

The wireless operator's seat consists of a simple metal sheet that is attached to the front edge of the main wing spar. It is normally fitted with a cushion to provide a basic degree of comfort for the wireless operator

The astrodome fits to the end of the cockpit canopy and is located above the wireless operator's position. It could be used either for the navigator to take fixing "shots" with his sextant or for the wireless operator to use his Aldis signalling lamp.

The Lancaster's main wing spar is massive and passes through the fuselage at a point behind the wireless operator's positions. It took much physical effort for the five airmen manning their positions ahead of the main spar to clamber over this obstruction, especially when wearing full flying gear.

The two emergency air bottles located on the rear starboard surface of the Lancaster's main wing spar provide separate air capacity for lowering the landing gear and the flaps, should the main system be disabled by battle damage. A battery would normally be housed below the step-frame.

The aircraft's reserve tank of hydraulic fluid is positioned on the port side of the main wing spar cover. It has a capacity of 7 imperial gallons. The disconnected flow pipe extends out from the rear of the tank. A black signal pistol in its circular metal "holster" is seen positioned alongside the tank

The Lancaster carries several heavy-duty axes for use in emergencies. This example on KB889 is mounted on the semi-bulkhead positioned on the port side of the fuselage between the wing spars.

The crew rest bunk in the Lancaster is positioned on the port side of the fuselage between the main and rear wing spars. The padding cover is dark green. The space beneath the bunk is normally utilized for storing oxygen bottles.

The metal cover for the Lancaster's flap operating cylinder and flap operating rods is located behind the rear wing spar cover, which can be seen at the top of the picture. Covers are sprayed interior green. The yellow electrical light cord is for display purposes and not a part of the aircraft.

The air filter unit fitted to late-production batches of the Lancaster is located on the right side of the fuselage. The equipment is housed inside a metal frame secured to the side of the fuselage.

The air filter unit mounted on the starboard side of the fuselage is seen in this forward view from the flap cylinder cover. The back support for the crew rest bunk is on the left and directly ahead of the wing rear spar. This view makes clear how difficult it was for the crew to move quickly through the center fuselage section, especially in an emergency.

A single stepladder frame, attached to the right side of the bomb bay bulkhead, provides access to the rear fuselage. Twin Plexiglas panels provide visual confirmation of whether or not all bombs have been released. The yellow electrical cord is for modern display lighting only.

The dinghy release cable is housed in a metal tube, which is sprayed red and mounted on the right side of the fuselage. Wording "DINGHY RELEASE – PULL CABLE HARD" is also red, and on a black background. A second release-point is located above the tail-plane main spar.

This is an example of the winching equipment used in loading RAF bombers. Trap doors in the bomb bay ceiling lifted up and the cables of the bomb carriers were attached to this equipment. The armorers then raised the bomb carriers into the bomb bay roof. The maximum safe load using the winch was 2,100 lbs, as marked on the large circular cover.

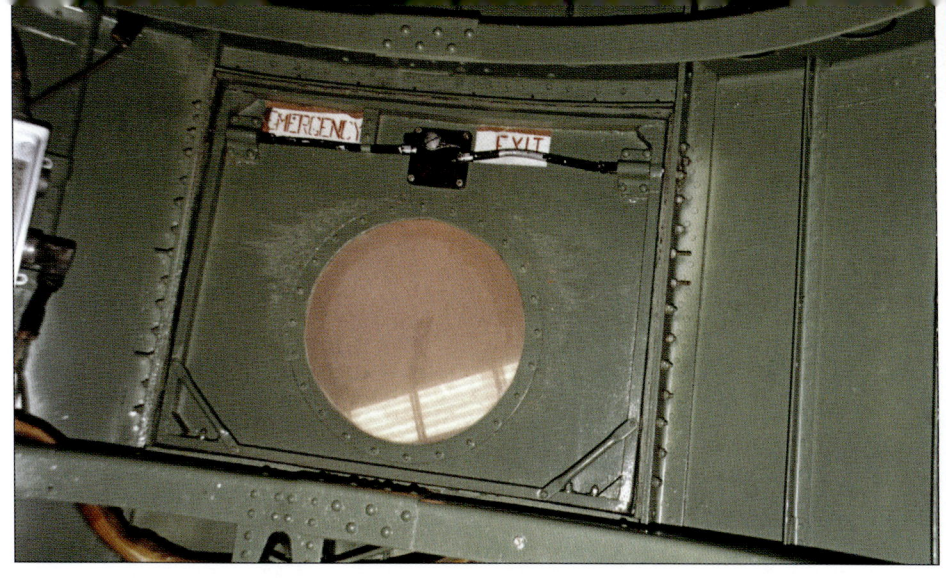

There are normally two crew emergency hatches on Lancasters, positioned in front of the mid-upper turret and between the wing spars. Each hatch is released by pulling on the black cable fitted to the rear edge. Wording "EMERGENCY EXIT" is applied in red. These exit points were primarily used when "ditching" or crash-landing. Seen here is the single hatch fitted on KB889, since the Martin turrets on the Mk. X Lancaster were fitted over the normal location for the rear hatch.

The Martin mid-upper turret is positioned over the bomb bay in KB889 and provides an easier access and exit for the gunner compared to the standard FN50 turret, which is positioned behind the bomb bay. The Martin turret was only installed in later-production batches of the Canadian-built Mk. X.

The ammunition boxes for the left-side pair of guns in the rear turret on KB889 are mounted on a small platform directly behind the bomb bay rear bulkhead. The boxes are retained in position by two vertical struts sprayed yellow. This arrangement was special to the Mk. X, since the starboard-side ammunition boxes on the Mks. I and III Lancaster were located over the end of the bomb bay.

All three of the gun turrets on the Lancaster were too constricted to permit air gunners to wear chest parachute packs. Pictured here is the parachute pack in its stowage pan for use by the mid-upper gunner, whose position is located on the right side of the rear fuselage.

The master compass unit is located directly ahead of the main entrance door and is mounted on a gimbal. The yellow frame consisting of two vertical and two horizontal segments is intended to prevent accidental disturbance of the compass unit. The "Keep Off" warning on lower frame is applied in red.

The black step-platform directly inside the main entrance door is supported by three struts sprayed interior green. The ammunition tracks for the left-side guns in the rear turret, when installed, are channelled under the step.

The standard five-rung ladder used for entry into and exit from the Lancaster is secured by three buckles mounted directly opposite the main entrance door on KB889. The ladder is sprayed black and has square angled base plates finished in silver

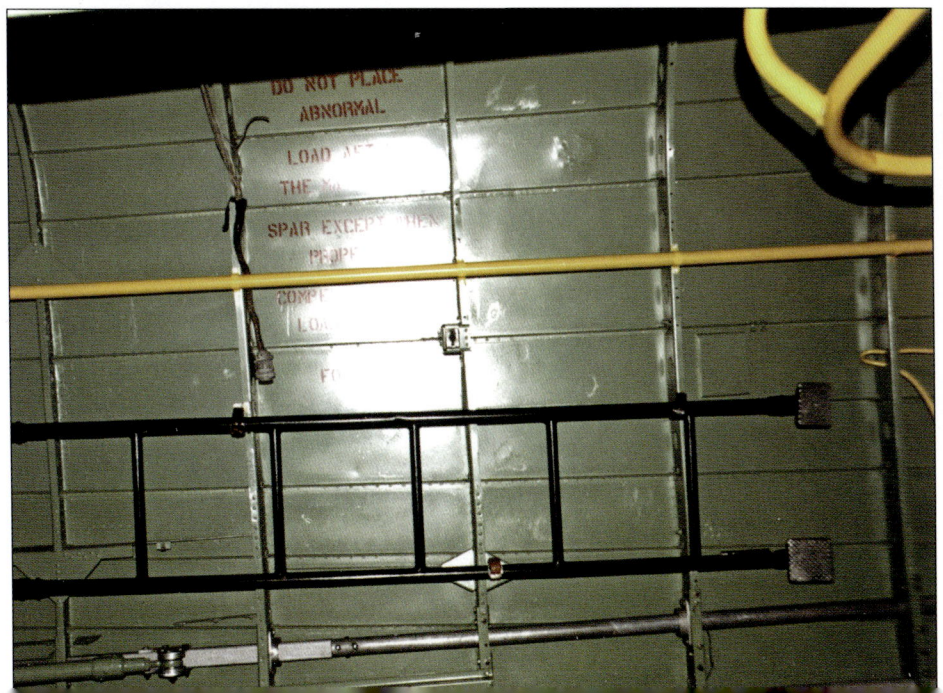

The flare chute on WWII British-built Lancasters was originally positioned up against the center of the bomb bay rear bulkhead. By contrast the flare chute on NX611 is located opposite the main entrance door. It is rectangular in shape, is mounted at a forward angle and has a large hinged cover. The unit is sprayed interior green.

The flare-chute aperture on PA474 is rectangular in shape and is fitted with a "blanking-off" cover plate, since it is no longer in use. The red circular fitting on the left is an Identification light

Propellers

Needle-bladed propellers

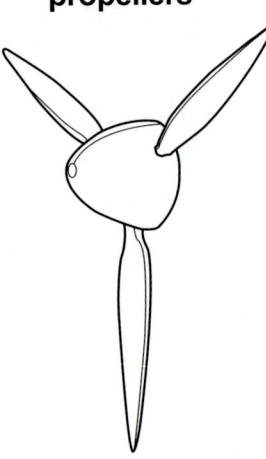

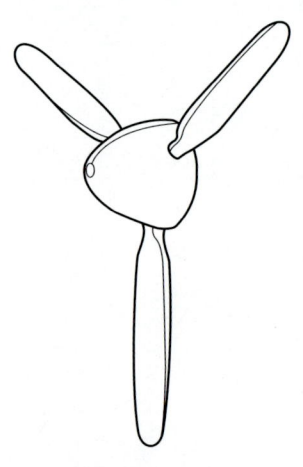

Paddle-bladed propellers

While operating the bomb sight in his compartment, the bomb aimer would be lying atop the main emergency escape panel. Visible here is the green leather pad on which the bomb aimer rested his upper body during this vital part of the entire "operation" or "op" (RAF term for a mission). PARACHUTE EXIT letters are in red on a white background.

Another heavy-duty axe is stowed on the starboard side of the fuselage ahead of the main entrance door. The axe head is red and its handle is black. Wording on the master compass unit at the top right of the picture states that the equipment is delicate and must be handled carefully.

The major interior color on Lancasters was a gray-green tone known as interior green and shown in this picture of the rear fuselage. The tail-plane sections are secured in place by four massive bolts. The actuator rod for the elevators enters the spar cover on the left side. Immediately in front of the spar is the Elsan chemical toilet.

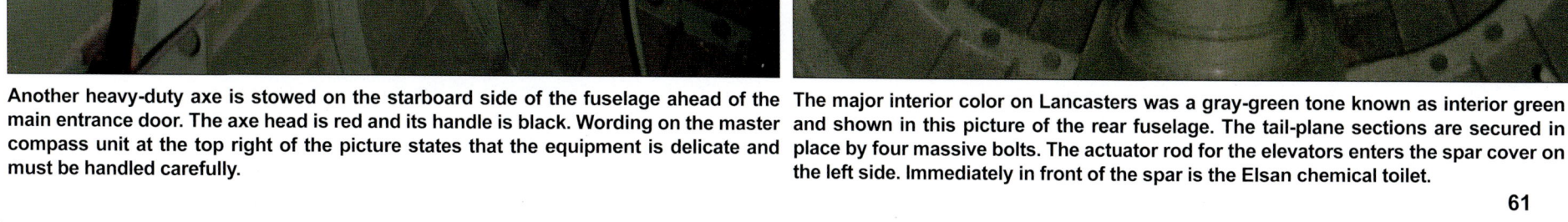

A few feet in front of the rear turret is a pair of plywood doors. A Plexiglas panel is fitted in the center of the right-side door. The rear gunner's parachute pack is stowed directly behind the door.

No. 617 "Dambusters" Sqdn. used these "bouncing bomb" aerial depth-charges to destroy the Möhne and Eder dams in May 1943. Their cylindrical shape allowed them to skip over the water's surface and then sink against the dam wall before exploding.

This is a standard mobile trolley accumulator in regular RAF service during WWII. Its use to start up an aircraft's engines was vital in saving the power resources on the aircraft itself. The unit is finished in what appears to be gray-green.

The left-side plywood door that closes off the rear turret from the main fuselage is seen in the shut position. Dark green padding in the center of the tail-plane main spar is intended to assist the gunner in moving smoothly to and from his isolated position.

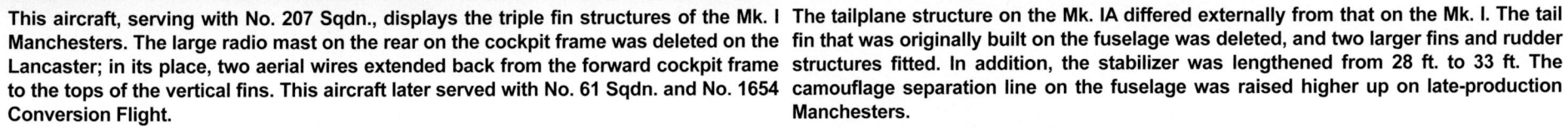

This aircraft, serving with No. 207 Sqdn., displays the triple fin structures of the Mk. I Manchesters. The large radio mast on the rear on the cockpit frame was deleted on the Lancaster; in its place, two aerial wires extended back from the forward cockpit frame to the tops of the vertical fins. This aircraft later served with No. 61 Sqdn. and No. 1654 Conversion Flight.

A Mk. I Manchester of No. 50 Sqdn. displays the revised camouflage separation line introduced in 1941. The fuselage line is angled up ahead of the central vertical fin. The picture also shows the FN7 mid-upper turret that became a standard item after the initial group of Manchesters were constructed.

The tailplane structure on the Mk. IA differed externally from that on the Mk. I. The tail fin that was originally built on the fuselage was deleted, and two larger fins and rudder structures fitted. In addition, the stabilizer was lengthened from 28 ft. to 33 ft. The camouflage separation line on the fuselage was raised higher up on late-production Manchesters.

The FN4A rear turret is here fitted on the second prototype Manchester L7247. The Plexiglas slopes down along the turret front in contrast to the more vertical framing used on the FN20 turrets later fitted to the Lancaster. This Manchester also has the three original vertical fins, with only the outer pair having rudders.

The second prototype Lancaster demonstrates how the dark-earth and dark-green upper camouflage pattern tends to merge with the countryside. The upper camouflage extends down the complete side of the aircraft. The engine exhaust staining is already beginning to show up. The yellow "P" in a circle denotes a prototype aircraft.

The "dustbin" shapes on trolleys are 4,000-lb. blast bombs known as "cookies," which became a standard weapon of RAF Bomber Command from 1941 onwards. The Mk. I Lancaster in the background features the original FN50 turret that did not have a tracking device to prevent the guns from inadvertently being fired into the fuselage or wings. KM codes (No. 44 Sqdn.) can faintly be seen beneath the OL codes for No. 83 Sqdn.

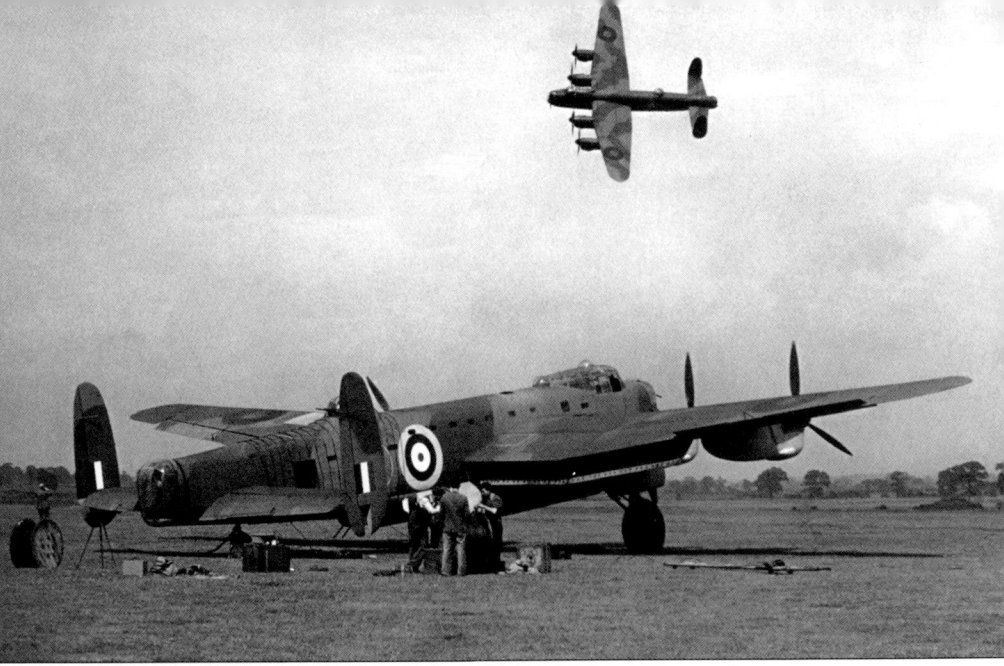

The underside gun turret on this prototype Lancaster is partially obscured from view by the right vertical fin. The turret was eliminated early in the Lancaster's operational career. The mid-upper turret has now been fitted with the tracking frame to prevent the gunner from inadvertently firing into the airframe. A production Lancaster banks steeply overhead.

The FN50 mid-upper turret is provided with a tracking device enclosed within the raised frame surrounding the turret base. The device ensured that the gun barrels kept clear of the aircraft's surfaces when the turret was rotating. A light-colored vertical fabric strip covers the junction point between the two rear fuselage sections.

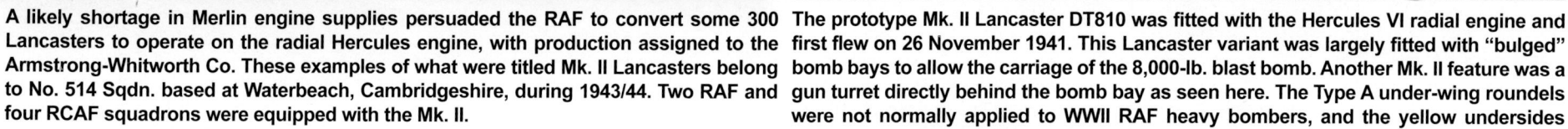

A likely shortage in Merlin engine supplies persuaded the RAF to convert some 300 Lancasters to operate on the radial Hercules engine, with production assigned to the Armstrong-Whitworth Co. These examples of what were titled Mk. II Lancasters belong to No. 514 Sqdn. based at Waterbeach, Cambridgeshire, during 1943/44. Two RAF and four RCAF squadrons were equipped with the Mk. II.

Lancaster Mk. II/DS704 demonstrates the aircraft's sound overall performance, with just one of the four Hercules XVI radial engines keeping the bomber aloft. This aircraft is seen prior to delivery to No. 408 "Goose" Sqdn. (RCAF) where it was coded EQ: W and finally went MIA over Frankfurt on 20/21 December 1943.

The prototype Mk. II Lancaster DT810 was fitted with the Hercules VI radial engine and first flew on 26 November 1941. This Lancaster variant was largely fitted with "bulged" bomb bays to allow the carriage of the 8,000-lb. blast bomb. Another Mk. II feature was a gun turret directly behind the bomb bay as seen here. The Type A under-wing roundels were not normally applied to WWII RAF heavy bombers, and the yellow undersides denote a prototype machine

The Hercules Mk. VIs of this Mk. II Lancaster are at full power as the pilot opens up. There are large-size spinner covers on the propellers. The slim air intake covers on the cowling tops were later replaced by larger-pattern shapes on the Hercules XVI.

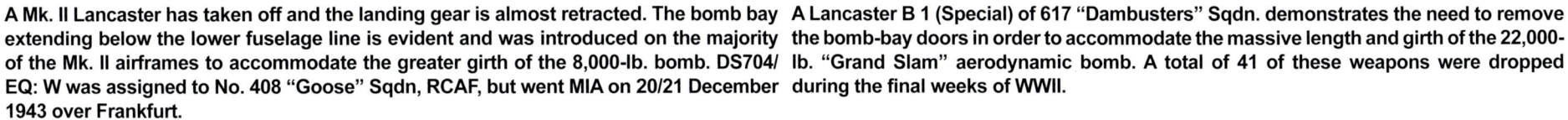

A Mk. II Lancaster has taken off and the landing gear is almost retracted. The bomb bay extending below the lower fuselage line is evident and was introduced on the majority of the Mk. II airframes to accommodate the greater girth of the 8,000-lb. bomb. DS704/EQ: W was assigned to No. 408 "Goose" Sqdn, RCAF, but went MIA on 20/21 December 1943 over Frankfurt.

A Lancaster B 1 (Special) of 617 "Dambusters" Sqdn. demonstrates the need to remove the bomb-bay doors in order to accommodate the massive length and girth of the 22,000-lb. "Grand Slam" aerodynamic bomb. A total of 41 of these weapons were dropped during the final weeks of WWII.

No. 75 (New Zealand) Sqdn. was based at Mepal in Cambridgeshire from June 1943 until VE-Day. This example bears the two parallel yellow bars on the outer fin/rudder assemblies. This marking denotes a G-H "leader" aircraft upon which other aircraft would form to conduct Pathfinder Force (PFF) daylight bombing operations. G-H was regularly used by No. 3 Group, within which No. 75 Sqdn. served.

B. Mk. I Merlin Engine

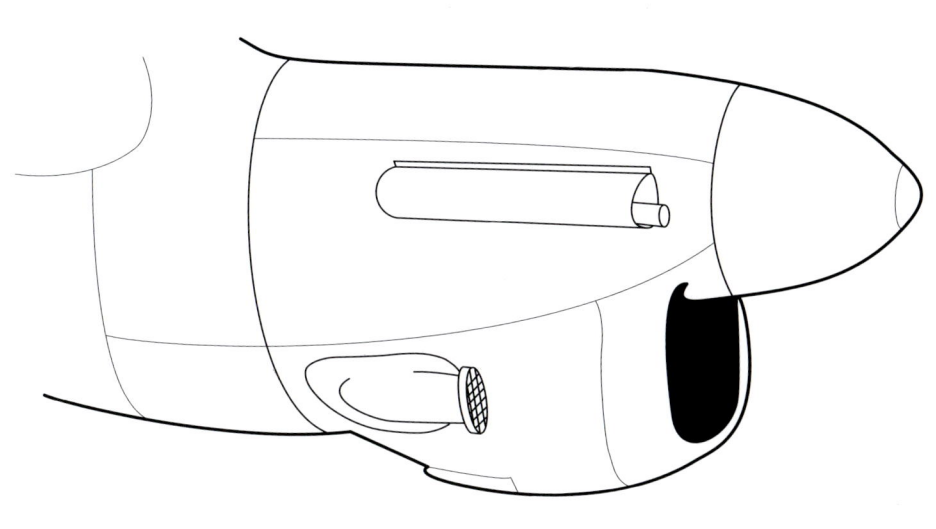

67

The tail fin structures on the Manchester Mk. IA differed from those on the Mk. I. The Mk. I's two small outer fins were replaced by larger units while the central fin was deleted. This Manchester Mk. IA joined No. 207 Sqdn. on 20 May 1941 but crashed on 1 September that year.

The Lancaster prototype was basically a Manchester airframe but the two Rolls Royce "Vultures" were replaced by four "Merlins" from the same manufacturer, and the Manchester's 90-ft. wing-span was increased to 102 ft. The maiden flight took place on 9 January 1941.

The Mk. I Lancaster dubbed *Our Willie* (SR: W/LL757) joined No. 101 Sqdn. at Ludford Magna, Lincolnshire, in April 1944. She is seen prior to being fitted with the three mast aerials for the ABC "Airborne Cigar" equipment that jammed Luftwaffe radio transmissions. *Our Willie* was declared MIA the following autumn.

The Mk. II Lancaster was equipped with Bristol Hercules radial engines. Early in its production run it was provided with "bulged" bomb bays in order to carry the 8,000-lb. "blast" bomb. This aircraft, belonging to No. 115 Sqdn, went MIA over Hamburg on 2/3 August 1943.

PB504 was the first of a production batch of 500 Mk. III airframes commencing May 1944. It was assigned to No. 49 Sqdn, and was regularly flown by F/Lt "Will" Hay, whose bomb aimer P/O Jack Mackay was the author's uncle. PB504 and the Hay crew all survived WWII.

This Canadian-built Mk. X first served at the Aeroplane and Armament Experimental Establishment (A & AEE) Boscombe Down, south of Amesbury in Wiltshire, as a trial machine for the Martin mid-upper turret during late 1944. It then saw active service with Nos. 428 and 419 (Canadian) Sqdns. and returned to Canada when WWII ended.

69

Sgt. John Mackintosh (pilot) discusses a problem on the main Engineer's panel with Sgt. Ron Sooley (flight engineer). Both were members of No. 207 Sqdn. based at Langar, Nottinghamshire, in mid-1943 Sooley's fold-up seat is directly behind the pilot's left arm, and the navigator's swivel seat is in the left foreground.

This veteran Mk. I Lancaster is W4783/AR: G, which served with No. 460. Sqdn, Royal Australian Air Force (RAAF) and is photographed at Binbrook, Linclonshire, during the early summer of 1944. The bomber flew 90 "ops" (missions) before being sent out to Australia. It now resides in the War Museum, Canberra.

Lancasters of No. 106 Sqdn. prepare to taxi out onto the perimeter track, ready for an "op" (mission) over Germany in late March 1944. The Sqdn, was based at Metheringham, Lincolnshire, at the time.

S for Sugar of No. 467, Royal Australian Air Force (RAAF) Sqdn. is being prepared for an "op." The bomber displays an impressive number of mission marks below the cockpit, and is fitted with the original bomb-aimer's Plexiglas cover and pitot-mast.

The true spirit of Bomber Command is exemplified by this picture. S for Sugar (R5868/PO: S) is about to fly her 100th "op" (mission) and the ground crew have chalked an appropriate message on the 8,000-lb. bomb.

The enemy was not responsible for all the hazards of operational flying. In this instance the rear turret on a Lancaster of UL: S2 from No. 576 Sqdn. has been totally chopped off, probably as a result of the impact of a bomb dropped by another aircraft on the same mission. The loss was probably more than material as well, since the rear gunner would not likely have survived such an incident.

Five air crewmen from No. 617 "Dambusters" Sqdn. pose in front of the stripped-out bomb bay of a Mk. I (Special) Lancaster. The massive shape and 22-ft. length of a "Grand Slam" aerodynamic weapon is slung in position. The 22,000-lb. bomb is further secured in position by a chain seen between the second and third airman from the right.

The winter of 1944/45 was particularly severe and provided great problems for the ground crews. In this instance the snow-shrouded airfield is Kelstern, Lincolnshire, which was home for No. 625 Sqdn. A tarpaulin covers the mid-upper gun turret on the Lancaster in the foreground.

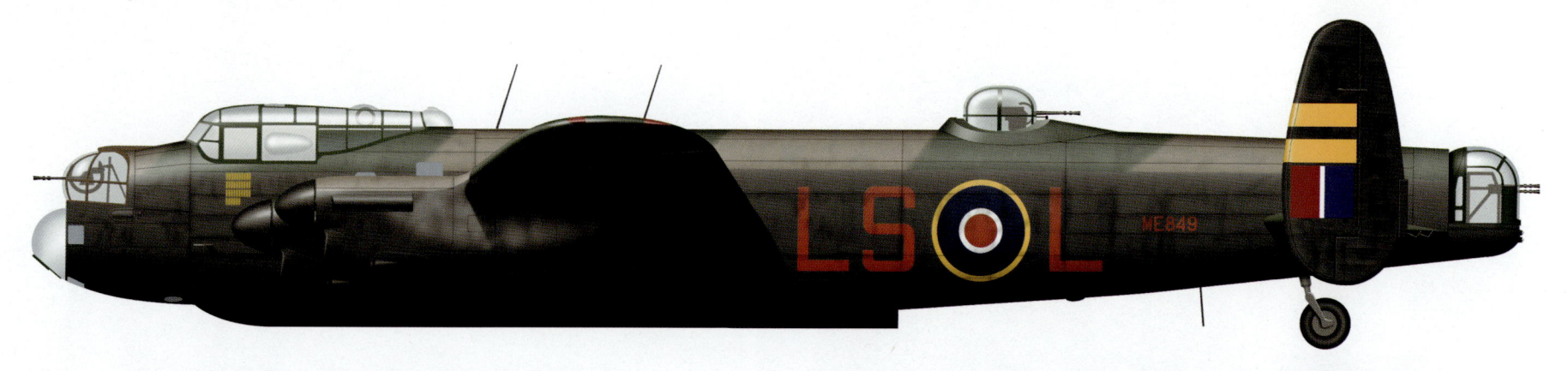

No. 3 Group used the blind-bombing device code named G-H during 1944/45. All aircraft so equipped bore two parallel yellow bars on their fins. The Mk. I Lancaster number ME849 served with No. 15 Sqdn. from June 1944 until the end of WWII.

Six Mk. III airframes were designated Mk. VI and equipped with the Merlin 87 with annular cowlings. Five went to No. 635 Pathfinder Force (PFF) Sqdn. ND673 flew operations between March 1944 and VE-Day and also served with the Royal Aircraft Establishment (RAE).

RF310 was one of the first Mk. III ASR Lancasters. It served with No. 1348 Flight in Burma (now Myanmar) but crashed taking off on 4 March 1946.

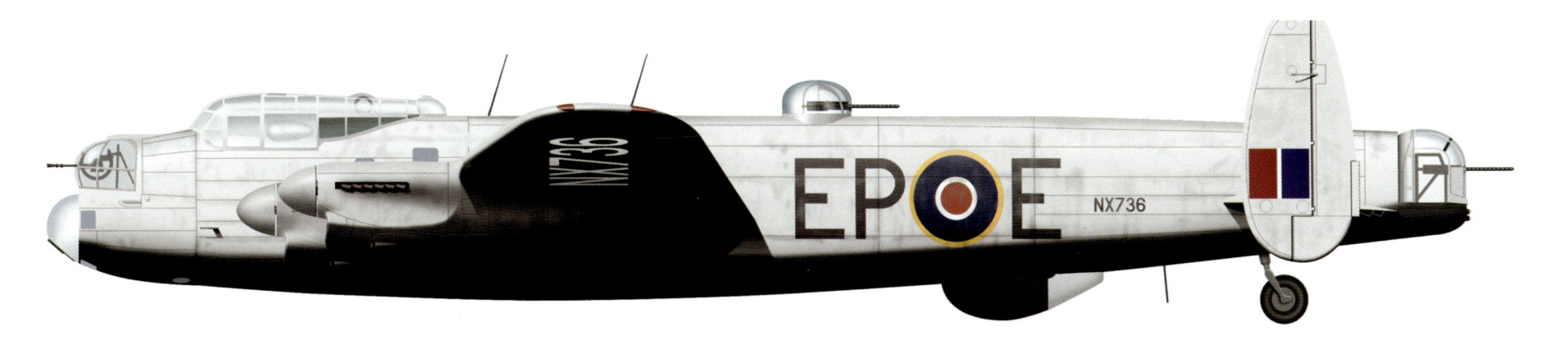

This Mk. VII Lancaster was modified for operations in the Far East in 1945. It served with No. 104 Sqdn. at Shallûfah, in Egypt's Suez Canal Zone, before being sent to No. 10 MU and "scrapped" during 1947.

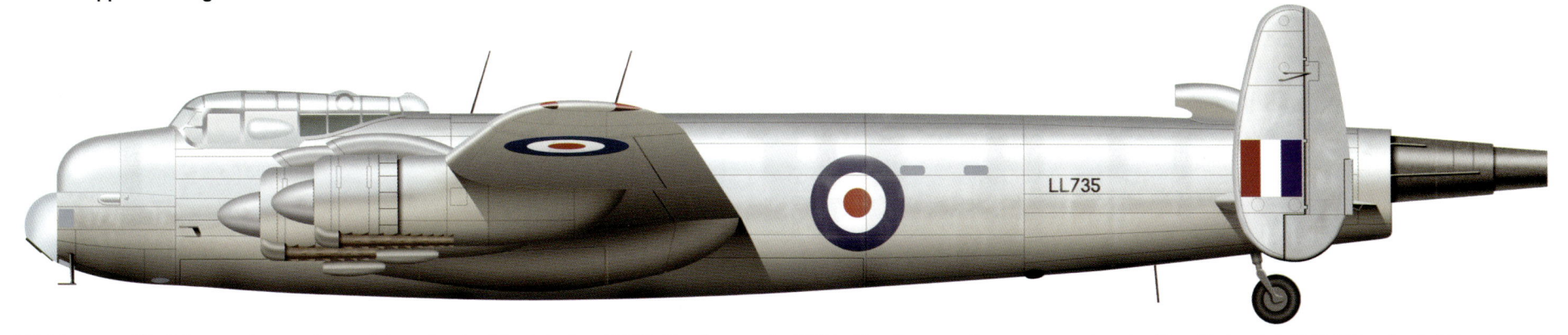

LL735 was a Mk. II Lancaster used as a jet-engine test-bed during WWII. She is seen in 1945 with all camouflage removed and with a Metrovick F2/4A Beryl axial-flow turbojet installed in the rear fuselage.

This Canadian-built Lancaster Mk. X, decked out in the final color scheme applied to Canadian Lancasters, served with No. 107 Rescue Unit at Torbay, Newfoundland, in 1956.

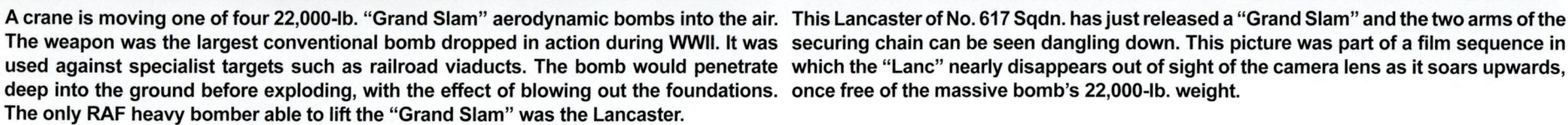

A crane is moving one of four 22,000-lb. "Grand Slam" aerodynamic bombs into the air. The weapon was the largest conventional bomb dropped in action during WWII. It was used against specialist targets such as railroad viaducts. The bomb would penetrate deep into the ground before exploding, with the effect of blowing out the foundations. The only RAF heavy bomber able to lift the "Grand Slam" was the Lancaster.

This Lancaster of No. 617 Sqdn. has just released a "Grand Slam" and the two arms of the securing chain can be seen dangling down. This picture was part of a film sequence in which the "Lanc" nearly disappears out of sight of the camera lens as it soars upwards, once free of the massive bomb's 22,000-lb. weight.

A Lancaster from No. 419 (Canadian) Sqdn. displays the classic pattern of engine-exhaust staining on the upper wing surfaces. Both outer engines threw out much lighter stain-patterns from their outer exhaust stubs, while the very light overall pattern created by the left-outer engine was another regular feature on the Lancaster.

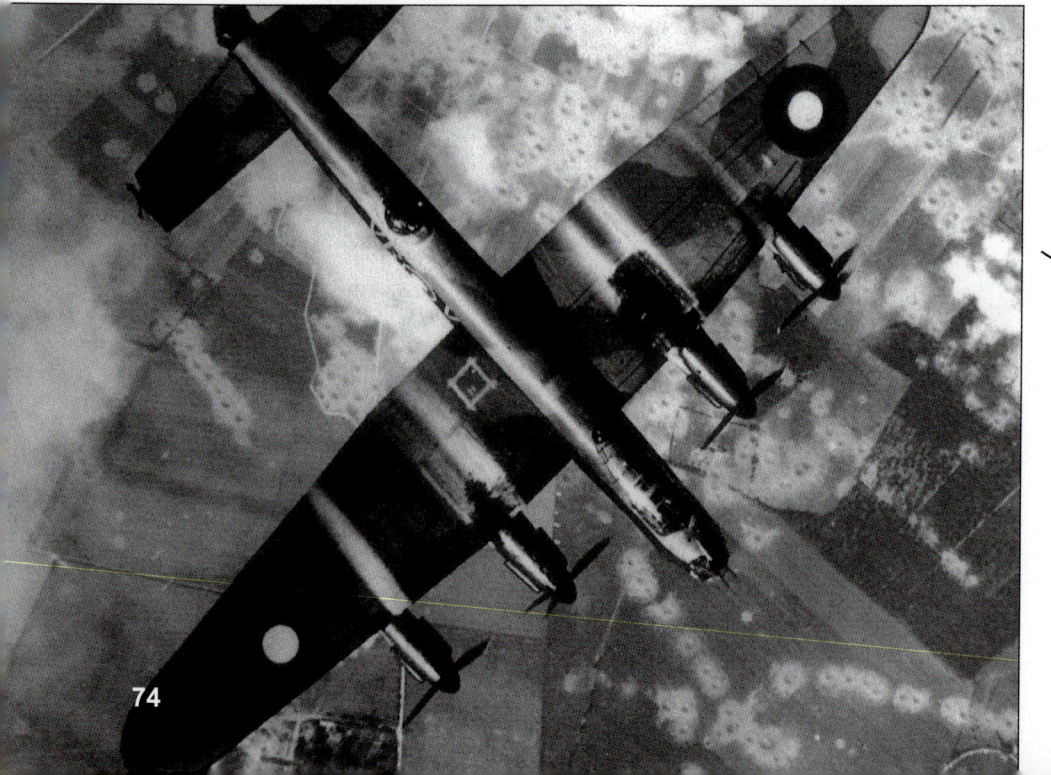

Hercules Engine Development

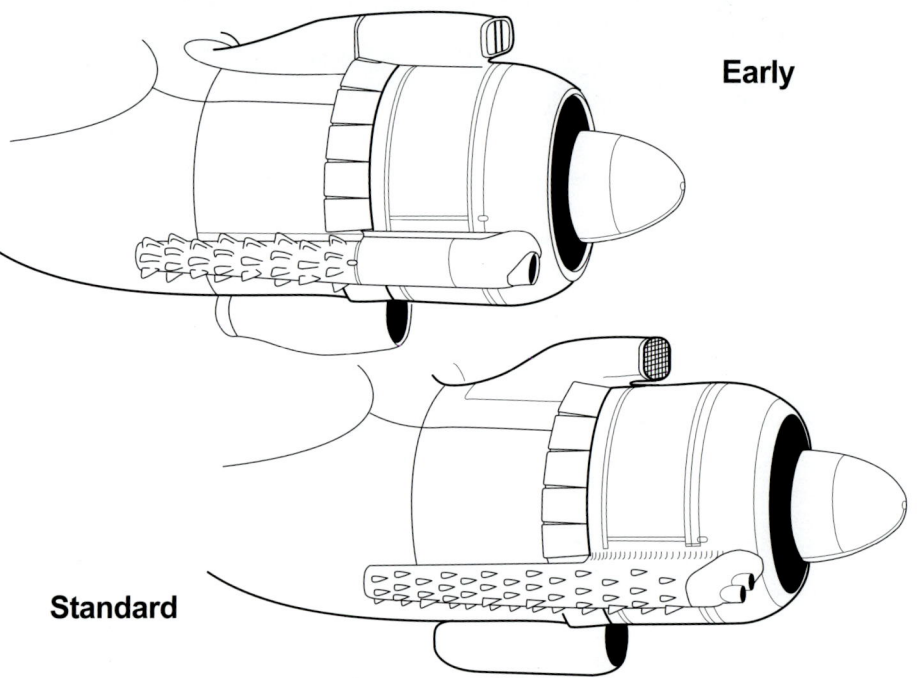

Early

Standard

This veteran Mk. I Lancaster has lifted off even before reaching the runway intersection. PM: M2 (known as "Mike Squared" or "Mother of them all") flew with No. 103 Sqdn. out of Elsham Wolds, Lincolnshire. The aircraft logged the amazing total of 141 operational sorties and survived WWII. It has the distinctive light exhaust staining that was a feature of weathering on Lancasters in particular.

This line-up of Mk. I, Far East (F.E.) Lancasters are preparing for a Goodwill Tour of the United States during 1946. The color-separation line on the engine cowlings is curved. Code letters are in red and Type C1 fuselage roundels and fin flashes can be seen. The upper wing surfaces bear Type C roundels, and the aircraft serial is applied in white under the wings.

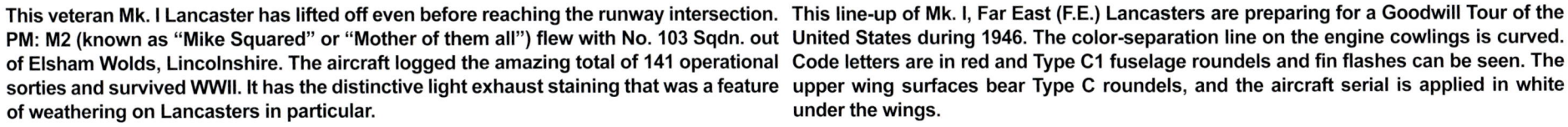

Cockpit Attachments

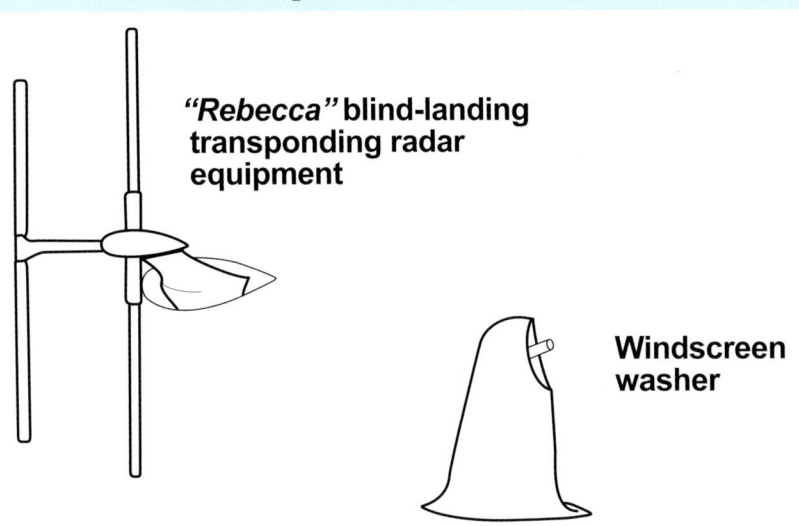

"Rebecca" blind-landing transponding radar equipment

Windscreen washer

A Mk. VII Lancaster believed to belong to No. 166 Sqdn. is photographed in an embarrassing position after a heavy emergency landing. The No. 1 engine has lost its propeller and the No. 2 propeller is thoroughly mangled. The bomber bears the standard Post-War scheme of white top and black under-surfaces. No. 166 Sqdn. was disbanded in late 1945.

The picture-angle of a Mk. VII Lancaster in flight gives a clear view of the black/white separation line. The FN50 mid-upper turret has given way to a Martin turret re-positioned further forward and equipped with two .50 caliber machine-guns. The air filter unit cover fitted to late batches of Lancasters is located above the starboard wing root. The aircraft belongs to No. 40 Sqdn. (BL) but only carries its aircraft letter. Type C wing and fuselage roundels and Type C1 fin flashes are applied.

As seen in this close-up view of the Martin mid-upper turret fitted on the Mk. VII Lancaster, the air gunner has an excellent field of view from the frameless Plexiglas cover. The circular shape on the top is a vent to allow fumes from the .50 caliber machine guns to escape when the weapons are fired.

A closer view of another FN82 rear turret on a Mk. VII Lancaster reveals how the .50 caliber gun barrels are fitted in heavy support frames. Also shown is the air-gunner's "clear vision" panel.

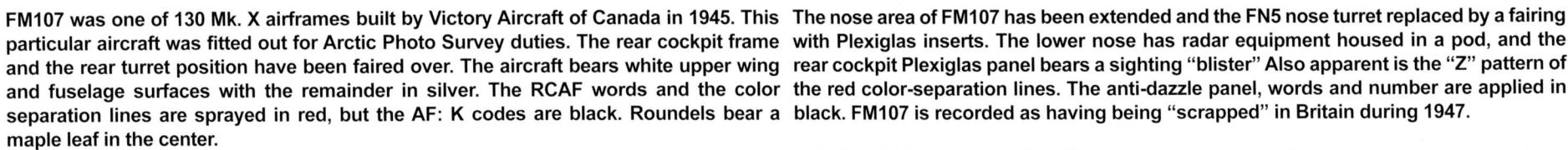

FM107 was one of 130 Mk. X airframes built by Victory Aircraft of Canada in 1945. This particular aircraft was fitted out for Arctic Photo Survey duties. The rear cockpit frame and the rear turret position have been faired over. The aircraft bears white upper wing and fuselage surfaces with the remainder in silver. The RCAF words and the color separation lines are sprayed in red, but the AF: K codes are black. Roundels bear a maple leaf in the center.

This Mk. X Lancaster retains the standard fuselage shape around the nose area as well as the color scheme for Maritime operating aircraft. The significance of the 889 serial applied to the wing, fuselage, and vertical fin lies in the fact that it is the same aircraft now resident at Duxford's IWM Museum on which this book is largely based.

The nose area of FM107 has been extended and the FN5 nose turret replaced by a fairing with Plexiglas inserts. The lower nose has radar equipment housed in a pod, and the rear cockpit Plexiglas panel bears a sighting "blister" Also apparent is the "Z" pattern of the red color-separation lines. The anti-dazzle panel, words and number are applied in black. FM107 is recorded as having being "scrapped" in Britain during 1947.

This Mk. CII Lancastrian VM733 was one of several airframes adapted to test various engines. In this case "Sapphire" jet-propelled units displace the outer engine nacelles. The normal Merlin engines were also used for test-comparisons between Rotol and De Havilland "paddle" blade propellers. The Mk. CII was an RAF variant intended for use as a long-range transport.

A Lancaster climbs out at CFB Trenton, Ontario, on 5 July 2009. It was headed home for Hamilton after attending the open house/airshow at Trenton. The VR: A markings commemorate the Lancaster on which P/O Andrew Mynarski (RCAF) won a posthumous Victoria Cross on 12 June 1944. (Rich Kolasa)

A Canadian Warplane Heritage (CWH) Lancaster banks for the crowd at Willow Run Airport in Belleville, Michigan, on 18 July 2009, during the "Thunder over Michigan" annual event. The Martin mid-upper turret on VR: A displacing the normal FN50 turret is the main external difference between British and Canadian-production Lancasters. (Rich Kolasa)

An Avro Lancaster B Mk. X owned by the Canadian Warplane Heritage Museum sits on the tarmac at "Thunder Over Michigan" in Willow Run, Michigan, in August 2006. (David Doyle)